# YOUR BRAIN'S POLITICS

How the Science of Mind
Explains the Political Divide

George Lakoff and
Elisabeth Wehling

**SOCIETAS**
essays in political
& cultural criticism

imprint-academic.com

Published in the UK by
Imprint Academic, PO Box 200, Exeter EX5 5YX, UK

Distributed in the USA by
Ingram Book Company,
One Ingram Blvd., La Vergne, TN 37086, USA

ISBN 9781845409210

A CIP catalogue record for this book is available from the
British Library and US Library of Congress

First published in German by Carl-Auer Publishers, Heidelberg,
Germany, 2008

To Kathleen
and
to Eve

# Contents

# A Note About This Book

Over the past decades, research in cognitive science and linguistics has uncovered astounding facts about the human mind. This is a dialogical introduction to these findings and their implications for politics.

Enjoy!

George Lakoff and Elisabeth Wehling
Berkeley, August 2016

# Chapter 1

# *Normal Thought*
## *Reasoning in Metaphors*

### 1.1. The Embodied Mind:
### Things we don't know about our reasoning

**Elisabeth Wehling (E.W.)** You once wrote that metaphors can start wars, and that the second Gulf War and Iraq War were largely motivated by metaphors.[1]

How on earth do cognitive linguists come to ascribe this much power to a harmless, rhetoric device?

**George Lakoff (G.L.)** It has to do with how our brains function. We all reason about the world largely in terms of metaphor. Metaphors are omnipresent, and not just in political discourse. They structure people's everyday language and reasoning.[2] And yes, metaphors have a firm grip on the political decision-making of individuals and of whole nations.[3] There is not a single political issue that we can reason about in entirely literal terms, without using metaphor. People's understanding of the world is largely metaphoric, day in and day out.

---

[1]  Lakoff 2003.

[2]  See Lakoff & Johnson 1980; see also, e.g., Bergen 2012; Boroditsky 2000; Gibbs 1994, 2006; Lakoff & Johnson 1999; Moeller et al. 2008; Zhong & Liljenquist 2006.

[3]  E.g., Lakoff 1996; Landau et al. 2009; Oppenheimer & Trail 2010; Schlesinger & Lau 2000; Thibodeau & Boroditsky 2011; for a review see Bougher 2012.

**E.W.** What is startling is the fact that folks don't know this, that they are completely unaware of this fact about their own reasoning. But then again, most people hold quite a few entirely false assumptions about how their minds work.

**G.L.** Exactly. Let's go through the four biggest mistaken assumptions about human thought.

First, people assume that thought is conscious. Well, that's wrong. Most thought, an estimated 98 percent, is completely unconscious.[4]

Second, a lot of us believe that human rationality is a thing that exists somehow independent of our bodies. That's also not true. Reasoning is a physical process that depends on our bodies and the physical realities of our brains.[5]

Third, many folks hold that reasoning is universal, meaning that all people reason in the same way. Wrong again. People do *not* all share one universal way of reasoning. They reason about the world differently, partly because their minds have acquired distinctive structures through their cultural and individual experiences.[6]

Fourth, people believe that humans can understand things as they "literally" exist in the world, and that they can talk about them in an objective way. Well, that's not true. We reason and speak in terms of metaphor all the time without noticing it. Abstract ideas, for instance, cannot readily be reasoned or talked about in any truly meaningful way without the use of metaphor.

Thus, in order to understand how metaphors define political thought and action—and how they can in fact lead to *warfare* between nations—we need to consider the basic mechanisms of human cognition. How do we understand the world around us on an everyday basis? Well, more often than not, in terms of metaphor.

---

[4]    E.g., Higgins 1996; Kahneman & Tversky 1984; Rock 2005; Thibodeau & Boroditsky 2011.

[5]    E.g., Barsalou 2008; Gallese & Lakoff 2005; Pulvermueller 2001, 2002; Niedenthal et al. 2005.

[6]    E.g., Boroditsky 2001; Boroditsky et al. 2003; Casasanto & Jasmin 2010; Casasanto 2014; Nuñez & Sweetser 2006.

**E.W.** That sounds nothing like the conventional under-standing of metaphors, which is that they are a matter of language and language only. Aristotle, for instance, described metaphor as an artistic form of language.

**G.L.** Most people think of metaphor as a matter of words and language, and that conception has spanned over 2,500 years of Western scholarship. But over the past four decades, cognitive science research has brought about ground-breaking findings that force us to change many of our traditional assumptions about how human language and thought work.

Today we know that metaphors are by no means a matter of "language and language only". Metaphors struc-ture our everyday cognition, our perception of reality. They are a matter of thought, they are a matter of language, and they are a matter of actions.

**E.W.** Our readers might say: Language? Sure. Thought? Maybe. But actions?

**G.L.** And from where do our actions emerge, if not from our thoughts?

**E.W.** Fair enough. Let's talk about the day that Conceptual Metaphor Theory[7] was born.

**G.L.** We are in the seventies. I'm a young professor, teaching at the Linguistics Department at the University of California at Berkeley. It's the spring semester and I'm teaching a course on metaphors. It's early in the afternoon. Outside, it's raining. We are in the San Francisco Bay Area, it rains all the time.

The students have spent the week reading some text or other on metaphors—that is, conventional metaphors—and we start class by discussing their reading notes. We are fifteen minutes into class when the door opens and a soaking wet student enters. She apologizes for being late, sits down,

---

[7]    Conceptual Metaphor Theory: Lakoff & Johnson 1980.

and opens her book. She seems distressed, and she is clearly struggling to hold herself together. But she doesn't say anything, and so we continue on with our discussion. Finally, it's her turn to share her reading notes. She starts talking, but after the first few words she breaks into tears. We look up at her, alarmed and concerned. I ask her what the matter is and she replies, sobbing, "I'm having a metaphor problem with my boyfriend. Maybe you can help. He says that our relationship hit a dead end street."

**E.W.** And so?

**G.L.** Well, let's remember now, this is the seventies. We're in Berkeley, at the university that is the home of the Free Speech Movement. We're in the San Francisco Bay Area and Berkeley is at the epicenter of the cultural revolution of 1968. In short, we are living in extraordinary times.

So, since we can tell that the student is going through a personal crisis, we embrace it, in the spirit of the time. We turn to a collective discussion of the crisis at hand.

We are a good way into this therapeutic group discussion, when we say, "Okay, look, your boyfriend says the relationship hit a dead end street. That means you can't keep going the way you're going. You may have to turn back." At this point, we realized that we were speaking of love in terms of travel. And we collected more and more examples: "It's been a bumpy road," "We're at a crossroads," and so on. And we realized that the metaphor was not in the words, it was part of the reasoning that lay behind all of the particular linguistic expressions.

**E.W.** The young man didn't use a metaphor just to break the news to his soon-to-be ex-girlfriend in a rhetorically aesthetic manner. His underlying reasoning was in terms of that metaphor.

**G.L.** Yes. In his mind a relationship was a vehicle that was supposed to help you go places in life, not take you to a dead end street. So when he felt that things were not *going* anywhere, he decided to *get out*.

**E.W.** He used a very common metaphor, namely *Love Is A Journey*. Many people use this metaphor when making relationship decisions.

**G.L.** And in his case, it meant ending a relationship that was *stuck*, that was not *getting* him anywhere.

**E.W.** What became of your student?

**G.L.** She is happily married, to another man.

### 1.2. Metaphoric Thought is Physical:
### How metaphors enter our brain

**E.W.** There's scientific evidence that we reason in terms of metaphors partly because of how our brains function. As we grow up, we automatically acquire a large number of so-called primary metaphors, without having consciously chosen any of them.[8]

**G.L.** Right. Take the *More Is Up* metaphor as an example. This metaphor is found throughout the world and across cultures. People speak of *rising* and *falling* prices. Stocks can go *through the roof* or be *in the basement*. Based on this metaphor, *more* is construed as *higher up* in space and *less* as *lower down* in space. And these mappings are asymmetric. We don't have the opposite mapping. We don't have a metaphor that construes *more* as *down*. We don't say, "Property prices are at an all-time *low*" to mean that property has become more expensive over the past years.

**E.W.** But it is merely in our minds that prices *rise*. In reality, they do no such thing. They become more or less, a phenomenon of quantity, not verticality, but we perceive them as *rising* or *falling* because our minds automatically apply the *More Is Up* metaphor.

The interesting question is, why, of all things, do we think about prices as moving around, up and down, and up

---

[8]　E.g., Lakoff & Johnson 1980; Grady 1997; C. Johnson 1997; M. Johnson 1987.

again? Why do we use a metaphor that construes quantity in terms of verticality?

**G.L.** The answer lies in our everyday experience. When you fill a glass with water, the *more* water you add, the *higher* the water level rises. When you put a stack of books on a table, the stack grows *higher* as you add *more* books to it. We all share this experience of seeing quantity correlate with verticality.

Quantity and verticality are processed in different parts of the brain. Verticality is processed in a region that has to do with physical orientation in the world. Quantity is processed in a region that handles numbers and masses. The two areas are not even next to each other in the brain. Yet there are neural connections between them.

**E.W.** Are we saying that all reasoning is metaphorical?

**G.L.** No. Take the example of the water level that rises as we add more water to the glass. Well, that water level in fact *rises*. We can say, "The water level has risen," and that is literal. That is not metaphoric. But when we say, "The prices have risen," or "Despite my diet my weight has not gone *down*," we are thinking and speaking in terms of a metaphor, a metaphor our brain acquired based on our experiences.

**E.W.** The experiences we make as we live in this world result in physical changes to our brains.

**G.L.** Yes. First off, all reasoning is physical. We understand the world via our brains, which are part of our bodies. Any reasoning process is always a *physical* process.

And metaphors, for instance, are engrained in our brain just like all other things that structure human thought.[9] The interesting question is, "What determines the structural details of our brains?" The answer is, in fact, "To a large part, our experiences in the world."

---

[9]     Boulenger et al. 2009; Citron & Goldberg 2014; Desai 2011; Gamez-Djokic et al. 2015; Lacey et al. 2012.

When we are born, there are a vast number of neural connections in our brains, connecting all sorts of neural clusters to each other. As we grow up between birth and the age of five or so, about half of those connections are lost.

**E.W.** Hold on, that sounds as if our capacity to think is reduced by half in the first five years of our lives.

**G.L.** Not at all. Our capacity to think is not being reduced. It is being formed. The right question to ask is not, "How *much* can we think," but rather, "In what *way* will we think?"

When we are born, we simply have this huge amount of random neural connections. Our brains are full of them. And as we grow older, half of them will be lost. And our world experience decides which connections we get to keep. Neural connections that get activated regularly through experiences during the first years of our lives get strengthened in the brain.

**E.W.** And those connections that are not regularly activated get lost, because there is no experiential basis for strengthening them.

The following picture emerges in my mind's eye: our experiences are like an invisible hand that reaches into our brain, molding it. And we have no clue that this goes on — it's automatic.

**G.L.** That is a good way to put it, yes. Our experiences structure the ways in which we reason. The more often we use any given synapse, the "stronger" a connection becomes, and the easier it is for the brain to activate the associated neurons.

Now, when two areas of the brain are active at the same time — like in the case of verticality and quantity that we discussed just a minute ago — those two regions grow strong synaptic connections. And via spreading activation along neural pathways linking those two regions, a neural circuit is formed. That circuit is the metaphor.

**E.W.** In the cognitive sciences, this mechanism is called "Hebbian learning."[10] Experiential correlations lead to strong neural and cognitive connections.

**G.L.** Yes. And so our cognitive apparatuses are heavily influenced by the experiences we make in our lives.

### 1.3. Metaphoric Thought is Inescapable:
### Not all arguments can be arguments

**E.W.** The implications of these neural processes for our perception of reality seem quite drastic. It sounds like people are not free to think in whichever way they desire. Instead, it is the physiology of our brains that determines how we think — and, moreover, what we simply *cannot* think!

**G.L.** That is factually true. Let's revise the example of the *More Is Up* metaphor. We reason in terms of this metaphor because we see verticality and quantity co-occurring on a daily basis. And thus our brains acquire a neural connection between the two concepts. Once this has happened, we will automatically and frequently reason about quantity in terms of verticality, whether we intend to do so or not. We have no conscious choice about this at all.

**E.W.** Every one of us automatically acquires a highly complex system of such conceptual metaphors. Some metaphors are simple in nature, like *More Is Up*. Others are complex in nature.

**G.L.** Let's first consider simple metaphors. A good example of a simple metaphor is the *Argument Is Physical Struggle* metaphor: you can *dominate* an argument. You can be *beaten* in an argument. You can *hit* your interlocutor with *strong* points. We *struggle* over the outcome of an argument.

**E.W.** Not so fast. An argument and a physical struggle de facto display a lot of parallels. To name just one, one person wins and the other person loses. Couldn't it be the case that

---

[10]   See, e.g., Caporale & Dan 2008; Hebb 1949; Shatz 1992.

we simply borrow language from the domain of fighting to have more vivid means of talking about arguments?

**G.L.** Not really. We talk about arguments in terms of physical struggle because we automatically *reason* about them in this way. How do we acquire this metaphoric mapping? Well, as a child, we experience the two domains simultaneously—over and over again. We argue with our parents and, at the same time, we struggle with them physically. I'm sure you can recall situations like this one: your mom wants you to do a certain thing, say, not run across the road to play with another child. She holds your arm and says, "No, stop, you're staying here." And while you're trying to shake her off, you lament, "But I wanna go play!"

Now, this simultaneous experience of physical struggle and verbal argument results in the formation of the simple metaphor *Argument Is Physical Struggle*.

**E.W.** People usually cite the *Argument Is War* mapping when it comes to metaphors for arguing. This construct has somewhat become a poster child for Conceptual Metaphor Theory.

**G.L.** Yes, there is a metaphoric mapping that construes argument in terms of warfare. For instance, we talk about *positioning* ourselves in an argument and we *battle* with words! So yes, the metaphor *Argument Is War* is very real. But it is just one special case of the metaphor *Argument Is Physical Struggle*.

**E.W.** "*Battling*" with words? Forgive me, but doesn't that seem a bit far-fetched.

**G.L.** Not so. We all conceptualize words metaphorically as weapons. We speak of *targeted* comments. We *aim* at something with our words, we *hit* someone with words, even *injure* them. And I'm sure you couldn't even put a number on how often you encouraged your students to speak by telling them, "All right, *shoot!*"

**E.W.** Let's look at the complex metaphor *Argument Is War* more closely. It's composed of multiple parts.

**G.L.** Yes. First of all, war itself is conceptualized metaphorically. In our reasoning, warfare between two nations is understood as physical struggle between two nations.

Obviously, nations cannot *actually* physically fight each other. But when we think about nationhood, we commonly apply the metaphor *Nations Are Persons*.

**E.W.** Nations *talk* to each other. They can be *friends* or *foes*. We speak of countries as our *neighbors*, and so on. Those are just a handful of linguistic examples for the *Nations Are Persons* metaphor.

**G.L.** And based on this metaphor, warfare is the physical struggle between two nation-persons. Now, add the metaphor *Argument Is Physical Struggle* and voila—we arrive at *Argument Is War*, with warfare standing in for one specific case of physical struggle.

**E.W.** Why not skip all those steps and simply go with *Argument Is*, well, *Argument*?

**G.L.** People are free to try. But they shouldn't get their hopes up. It's literally impossible to avoid metaphor in our language and reasoning. We cannot disregard the physical realities of our brains. We simply cannot wake up one day and say, "I will no longer reason in terms of metaphor," because metaphoric reasoning is automatic. In our brains, we *struggle* with each other as we argue. That's the point. So, to return to your proposition—no, we cannot simply think of argument as nothing more than argument, just as we cannot simply think of quantity as nothing more than quantity. We all share certain experiences as human beings in this world, and those experiences force our brains to acquire certain metaphoric mappings.

**E.W.** Still, many people believe that things can be denoted in a literal way, just as they exist in the world, and that metaphor muddies the water in communication. John Locke once asserted: "Metaphors must without question be entirely avoided in any discourse that claims to inform or teach the listener; whenever truth and knowledge are concerned, they ought to be considered a grave misstep, either of language itself or of the person that utilizes them."

**G.L.** Notice Locke's metaphors. He metaphorically construes action as motion when saying it's a "misstep". And he metaphorically construes language as an instrument when saying a person "utilizes" it.

Locke assumed that reality per se exists in the world, independent of our conceptual systems. He held that we could perceive things as they objectively exist, that we could speak and reason in purely literal terms.

These assumptions about an objective reality are wrong. We perceive the world through a myriad of mental mechanisms, such as conceptual metaphors. We cannot understand things in this world in a disembodied, objective way. That thing we call "reality" is dependent not just on the nature of things in the world, but also the nature of our brains and bodies.[11] We understand countless concepts via metaphoric mapping mechanisms developed by our brains over time.

**E.W.** Reasoning about rather abstract ideas, for instance, is nearly impossible without metaphor.

**G.L.** Right. Take the notion of affection. We refer to people who are generally kind to others as *warm*-hearted. We speak of someone's *cold* heart. You can *warm up* to people you just met, and sometimes it takes a lot of time to get *warm* with someone. Relationships between people can *cool off*. And so on.

As you can see, we process the somewhat abstract notion of affection via metaphor, namely, the *Affection Is Warmth* metaphor.

---

[11] E.g., Barsalou 2008; Gallese & Lakoff 2005; Lakoff & Johnson 1999; Pulvermueller 2002; Niedenthal et al. 2005.

**E.W.** And we do this because of experiences we make already as infants. Every time our parents held us in their arms, we experienced physical warmth and affection together. And so in our brains, the regions for computing temperature and emotion were repeatedly activated simultaneously. Our "embodied mind" has learned a connection between the two concepts, because they constantly co-occur in our experience.

**G.L.** Right. And even though those regions are not even next to each other in our brains, we "learned" a neural connection between them through this recurring experience. This is far from being a rational choice, and we don't even notice this as it happens. It just happens. It is unavoidable.

**E.W.** And the same goes for the metaphor *Argument Is Physical Struggle*. We don't consciously decide to reason about arguments in terms of physical fights.

**G.L.** We certainly don't. We use this metaphor entirely automatically. It's part of our everyday unconscious reasoning.

### 1.4. Metaphoric Thought is Unconscious: Our mind's very private contemplations

**E.W.** You just said, "Metaphor is part of our everyday unconscious reasoning." That statement is bound to raise eyebrows with more than a few of our readers, "Everyday unconscious reasoning? Well, I don't know about you guys, but *I* know what I think!"

**G.L.** We have to disappoint those readers. It's safe to say that people do *not* know what they think[12] most of the time — about 98 percent of the time. That is, roughly, the percentage of human reasoning that remains unconscious to us.

**E.W.** "Unconscious thought" in a Freudian sense would imply that we couldn't ever access those parts of our

---

[12]  E.g., Higgins 1996; Kahneman & Tversky 1984; Rock 2005; Thibodeau & Boroditsky 2011.

reasoning. How can metaphoric mappings guide our everyday perception of the world if we are not even able to access them?

**G.L.** Unconscious thought as the cognitive sciences define it has nothing to do with Freud's notion of the unconscious. In cognitive science, the unconscious mind simply denotes all the parts of our reasoning that we don't notice, don't reflect upon, and cannot control.

**E.W.** One would think we need insight into our own thoughts in order to keep them clear and in order. How can we grasp our own ideas if we're not fully conscious of them?

**G.L.** The right question to ask is, "How could we ever manage to understand all the mental and neural mechanisms that guide our thoughts?"

You just asked me how we could *grasp* ideas without being aware of their mental structure.

As you posed that question, did you consciously reflect upon the fact that you were using the *Ideas Are Objects* metaphor? That by *grasping* ideas you become a metaphoric agent that *handles* ideas as metaphoric objects. Were you aware that we use this metaphor when we call some ideas easy to *grasp*, when we speak of *exchanging* ideas, or when we *bury* bad ideas?

Did you consciously think about the fact that ideas may also be understood in terms of other metaphors, such as *Ideas Are Food*—a metaphor that guides expressions, such as *chewing* hard on ideas, *swallowing* ideas, *digesting* ideas, or giving *feed*back?

Or did you consciously consider using yet another metaphor, such as *Ideas Are Locations*? This metaphor guides expressions such as *jumping from* one idea *to* another, *arriving at* good ideas, *distancing* oneself *from* bad ideas, and *approaching* solutions.

Did you deliberately ponder all of those options? I don't think so. We would have had to wait for a long time for you to formulate your question!

**E.W.** But if people were to invest that time, technically, they could arrive at a conscious understanding of the conceptual mechanisms they usually remain unaware of. After all, this is what we do in cognitive science research, which studies the unconscious part of human everyday cognition and language.

**G.L.** Sure. You can analyze the complex system of concepts and mechanisms behind people's communication, decision-making, and general perception of reality, which is what cognitive science research does—and we begin to understand that complex system more and more.

### 1.5. Metaphors Don't Come Alone:
### The many different ways to reason about things

**E.W.** We just discussed a number of different metaphors we commonly use when reasoning about our own reasoning. Ergo, we can have multiple metaphoric mappings for one and the same idea, for one and the same object, action, feeling, or whatever else.

**G.L.** We can indeed, because there are manifold experiences that correlate with each other. As an example, let's consider the notion of purposeful action, metaphorically speaking: the type of action that *gets you to where you want to be* or *gets you the things you want to have.*

**E.W.** When we use the first metaphor, we construe the purposes of our actions as geographic destinations and our actions as movement towards such destinations. This is called the *Purposes Are Destinations* metaphor. Now, the interesting question is, why do we use this metaphor?

**G.L.** Well, we all know what it's like to want to get from one location to another, from a starting point to a destination. Say you are a child, and you want your blanket, which is in the kitchen. To get your blanket, you have to go to the kitchen. Once you arrive at the kitchen, the purpose of your action has been fulfilled or — metaphorically speaking — your *goal* has been *reached*. Every day there are purposes that can only be fulfilled by moving towards a destination. This is how we acquire the metaphor. And this experience of moving towards a destination with purpose gets generalized and applied to all kinds of purposeful action. We say, "I *reached* my career *goals*," and mean by that: the purpose of my actions has been fulfilled.

**E.W.** A whole set of expressions falls out of this mapping: I have not yet *arrived* at my goals. I *took* many *detours* before *getting to* my goal. I overcame many *hurdles* in my career. I had to *get around* many *obstacles on my way* to the top. I *reoriented* myself towards a more balanced lifestyle. I got *ahead* in life. And so on.

But we said there are two metaphoric mappings for purposeful action. What about the second one? Why do we think and talk about the goals of our actions as objects?

**G.L.** We all share the experience of wanting an object. Let's say you are a child and you want your teddy bear, which is sitting on a shelf. Your demonstrably point to the bear so your parents will notice. Maybe you cry, whatever it takes. And then, once you hold the teddy bear in your arms, the purpose of your actions—pointing and crying—is fulfilled. Your brain learns a mapping between purposeful action and object acquisition. This is why we say things like, "I *got* what I wanted in life," to express that the purpose of our action has been fulfilled. We can *pocket* a success. We can *reach* high in life, and sometimes our goals are *far-fetched*. We can *lose* our *grip* on things, and we can make the wrong decisions and thereby *throw away* our career or marriage.

Bottom line, one and the same thing can be reasoned about in terms of two or more different metaphoric mappings. That is very common.

**E.W.** Right. Love, for instance, is an abstract concept that plays a huge role in our lives. Think of all the decisions that are being made around the world based on how we reason about love—whether they turn out to be the right or the wrong decisions, they are largely dependent on the metaphors that people resort to in order to reason about love.

Love has many different metaphors. There is *love as a journey* towards shared life goals. There is *love as a partnership* with shared burdens and gains. There is *love as becoming one unit*. There is *love as an invisible power* that functions as a connection between two people. There is *love as heat*, which is why we sometimes speak of love having grown *cold*. And so on. All these metaphors have different experiential bases in our lives.

**G.L.** And some of those metaphors seem to be shared across many cultures, while others are not.

### 1.6. The Cultural Brain: Why humans cannot all think alike

**E.W.** You're making an important point. Not all metaphoric mappings are shared by all humans.

**G.L.** Exactly. Only those metaphors are shared across many cultures that we learn on the basis of how the human body functions in the world, that is, what all our bodies have in common in terms of how they function in the world.[13] *Anger Is Heat*, for instance, is learned by all humans. We all share the basic experience of our body temperature rising, as we get angry. The feeling of anger and the increase in body temperature correlate, the two relevant brain regions are activated at the same time, and the neural connection gets strengthened — voila!

**E.W.** But this fundamental, largely culture-independent mechanism is not true for all metaphors. People grow up in different cultures, and they gain different cultural and subcultural experiences. And thus they learn different metaphors. Societal experiences can impact metaphor acquisition quite strongly.[14]

---

13    E.g., Lakoff & Johnson 1980.
14    E.g., Boroditsky 2001; Boroditsky et al. 2003; Meier et al. 2007; Nuñez & Sweetser 2006; Oppenheimer & Trail 2010.

**G.L.** Right, this is true for love, for instance. Different cultures have different mappings for this concept. Let's take *Love Is A Journey*. This is a complex metaphor that rests on a couple of smaller mappings. For instance, a relationship is understood as a vehicle. That mapping is omnipresent in language. Their marriage has *run aground*: the relationship as a boat. Their marriage has *derailed*: a train. Their marriage is *spinning its wheels*: a car. Why this mapping? Because a vehicle is something we use to move from one place to another. Thus, if you have shared life goals, you can jointly move towards them in the "relationship vehicle." And notice that another mapping is relevant here, namely, *Life Purposes Are Geographical Destinations*. If you take those two elements together, you start to see why we speak of relationship difficulties as difficulties in movement: a couple can overcome *obstacles* and find their *way* together, and others divorce because they find they're *going* in opposite *directions*.

**E.W.** So when people start relationships with each other, what they really do, cognitively speaking, is get into a car, board a train, or get aboard a ship.

**G.L.** No doubt. And some might even board a space shuttle, a submarine, a hot-air balloon, or a gondola. The metaphor *Relationship As Vehicle* is ubiquitous. It's not the only metaphor for relationships, but it is highly common in many cultures.

**E.W.** But why a vehicle, one might ask. Why can't we just move towards common life goals by foot?

**G.L.** There are a couple of reasons. First, a vehicle is a container. And relationships are commonly metaphorically processed as containers. We get *into* a new relationship, we stay *in* relationships, and we get *out of* relationships. The metaphor *Relationship As Container* is a very basic one. And vehicles—as a type of container—naturally match this construct.

Second, vehicles are containers with confined space, where passengers are physically close to each other. Well,

*Intimacy Is Closeness* is one of our core mappings when it comes to reasoning about human relationships. People in a relationship can be *close*, they may drift *apart*, and they may *distance* themselves from each other.

**E.W.** So if a friend says, "My girlfriend and I have never been as *close* as after her accident last year," then he uses the *Intimacy Is Closeness* metaphor. He does not mean to say that they never sat closer to each other on the couch when watching TV, and he does not mean to say they never slept closer to each other in their bed. What he is saying is that they never were more intimately connected to each other.

**G.L.** Right. Now, why do we have this mapping? Because, when we are children, we learn that people we intimately know are also physically close to us. Our parents hold us in their arms. Our siblings share a room with us. The whole family lives in one house. These are the types of experiences that result in the *Intimacy Is Closeness* metaphor.

Now, all these metaphoric elements come together in the complex metaphor *Love Is A Journey*: a relationship is a vehicle where two people sit close to each other and move towards shared life goals together.

**E.W.** If *Love Is A Journey* is not exclusively grounded in direct physical experiences, then there should be people who do not know this metaphor at all, people who are not able to reason in terms of this metaphor even if they wanted to.

**G.L.** That's right. There are in fact people who aren't familiar with the metaphor *Love Is A Journey*, for the following reason. In order to—metaphorically—move towards life goals together, you first need the notion of having such things as life goals. And while this may be surprising for some people, we know of cultures that do not construe the meaning of life as pursuing and reaching goals. And, in those cultures, there simply are no foundations for acquiring a metaphoric mapping along the lines of *love as a journey towards shared life goals*.

**E.W.** And that's not the only reason why some people don't develop this mapping. There are cultures in which women are extremely subordinated to men, and in those cultures a metaphor that construes love as a journey towards a shared life goal doesn't fly, for obvious reasons: only the husbands get to make decisions about life goals. The wife merely follows along. In this cultural context, a metaphor that construes love as a journey towards shared life goals is nonsense.

**G.L.** No doubt about it. So, bottom line, societal experiences can strongly impact which metaphors will become the conceptual foundations of our everyday lives – and which metaphors will be inaccessible to us. And if we have cultural differences in metaphor, we probably have culture-dependent differences in brain structure.

## 1.7. The Secret Selectors:
### How metaphors determine what we *don't* think

**E.W.** Let's talk about how metaphoric cognition impacts our perception of things in detail.

**G.L.** Have you ever been to Athens?

**E.W.** Yes.

**G.L.** Did you take a close look at the busses they have there?

**E.W.** Busses, as in public transport?

**G.L.** Yes.

**E.W.** No.

**G.L.** Aha. Let me tell you, then, what is written across busses in Athens, "metaphoroi". The word "metaphor" stems from Greek and literally means, "to carry things to another place." Metaphoric cognition, thus, means that we resort to elements from one cognitive domain – commonly one that we can directly experience in the world – in order to reason about another cognitive domain—commonly one that is more abstract.

**E.W.** In cognitive linguistics, the two are labeled source domain and target domain. Semantic elements and relational structures from the source domain are being mapped onto the target domain. And this conceptual process is called metaphoric mapping.[15] It's important to point out, though, that not *all* elements from one given source domain are being mapped onto the target domain.

**G.L.** Right, because if all elements were mapped from one domain to the other, we would no longer be looking at two conceptual domains, but merely at *one* concept! Metaphoric mappings are not exhaustive in the sense that all elements and relational structures are mapped from domain A to domain B.

**E.W.** And this is one of the most interesting and intriguing things about metaphors: they have a restrictive component to them.

**G.L.** Yes. Whenever we use one given metaphor in our language and reasoning—instead of using, say, another available metaphor or non-metaphoric structures—we restrict our understanding of the target domain to the structures that are provided by the source domain. And at the same time, the structure provided by the source domain profiles certain aspects of the target domain. Thus, metaphors both *hide* and *highlight* things that are inherent to the target domain.

**E.W.** This selective nature of metaphoric cognition has considerable implications for our perception of reality.

**G.L.** Exactly, because the metaphors we use determine what aspects of any given issue we will focus on—and what aspects our minds will simply ignore.

---

15    Lakoff & Johnson 1980.

### 1.8. We Do as We Think:
### Acting out metaphors

**E.W.** A moment ago, we said that metaphors are a matter of thought, language, and *action*. How about an example for the ways in which metaphors influence joint societal action?

**G.L.** Let's take the concept of morality. Morality is an essential driving force in politics. On top of that, morality is an abstract concept, a concept that our minds naturally and unconsciously process in terms of metaphoric mappings.

There are quite a few different metaphors for morality. One way to reason about morality is in terms of the Moral Accounting metaphor.[16] This metaphor builds on our experiences with well-being. By the way, this is a general phenomenon. All our metaphoric reasoning about morality is grounded in experiences with well-being, in the following way: things that maximize well-being are "good" or "moral"; things that minimize our well-being are "bad" or "immoral."

Now, let's look at the origin of the Moral Accounting metaphor. Our experience in life is that we are better off when we have the things we need. We thus have the metaphor *Well-Being Is Wealth*. And when you combine this general metaphor with the notion of accounting, you arrive at metaphoric moral accounting, in the following sense: maximizing well-being through moral action is conceptualized as an increase in wealth, and minimizing well-being through immoral action is conceptualized as a decrease in wealth.

**E.W.** That reasoning underlies many of our everyday expressions. If someone has done us a favor, we *give* a favor *back* later on. Until we do so, we have a moral *debt*. We *owe* that person a favor. And so on. Now, the crucial thing is that we do not just reason and talk about morality in this way, but also *act* based on the metaphor. But what if the opposite

---

[16]    Lakoff 1996.

happens and instead of doing favors for each other, people *harm* each other?

**G.L.** Okay, now this is interesting. There are different ways in which people may reason and talk about harm, and then act accordingly. For one, a person that did something bad can balance the books by doing something good in return. Thus, there's a concept of moral restitution, a notion that immoral deeds can be balanced via moral *reparation*: when you did something bad, do something good that weighs in at about the same level, and moral order is restored.

But there is also another inference that emerges from the Moral Accounting metaphor. That inference leaves us with quite a different story, and here is how that story goes: a person that did something bad receives a *payback* from the others. Harm is inflicted on the wrongdoer to compensate for the harm he or she has done, and this balances the moral books. This is the concept of moral retribution. And then there's revenge, which is more complex. It uses a form of moral arithmetic in which taking something good away from people is the equivalent of doing something bad to them. This is a metaphorical version of literal accounting, in which removing a credit is imposing a debit. This is how revenge cultures work.

**E.W.** In other words, if someone *takes a piece* of your well-being, you have two options. You can have that person *restore* your well-being by doing something good for you. Or, you can *take a piece* of their well-being by doing something bad to them.

**G.L.** Yes. And in both cases we *balance the books*, or get *even*. Which is understood as a form of justice.

**E.W.** And if we fail to do so we are left with a *debt* to settle.

**G.L.** Exactly. As you see, the ways in which we reason about morality are entirely dependent on metaphor. When people deal with moral issues, they commonly use the Moral Accounting metaphor. Whether they follow the concept of restitution or the notion of retribution, the books must be balanced. Immoral deeds must be *paid for*—in one way or another.

## 1.9. The Public Brain:
### Metaphors in political discourse

**E.W.** We already talked about the selective mechanism of metaphors, the fact that they both *hide* and *highlight* realities. The implications of this for political reasoning are huge: metaphors used in public discourse can determine what people think—and what they ignore!

**G.L.** Right. All the things in the world that we reason about —actions, objects, emotions, policy issues, and so on—can be construed in terms of not just one, but many different source domains. However, those different source domains are never used simultaneously. Rather, our minds have to choose one of them.

**E.W.** And here is where it gets interesting: this "choice" is usually entirely unconscious. It's simply not the case that we look at abstract concepts, such as taxation, and ask ourselves, "What source domain for taxation should I use today?"

**G.L.** Right, but if the choice is not conscious and deliberate, then how *is* that choice being made? Well, to a great extent, it's the language that is used in public discourse that determines how things are perceived. Metaphoric language evokes metaphoric structures in our minds, and those structures will guide our understanding of a given thing or situation.[17]

**E.W.** And since different metaphoric source domains will always both highlight and hide *different* aspects of the thing we reason about, metaphoric language has a huge impact on our perception of reality—both in everyday life and in politics.

---

[17]   E.g., Lakoff 1996; Landau et al. 2009; Schlesinger & Lau 2000; Thibodeau & Boroditsky 2011; for a review see Bougher 2012 and Wehling 2013.

**G.L.** But that's only one part of the issue. There is more to this. Namely, the more often a metaphoric mapping is used in language, the more that metaphor is being engrained in people's brains due to synaptic strengthening.[18]

If public political debate implements one given metaphor again and again—then that metaphor becomes our primary way of perceiving the issue at hand. The mapping simply becomes part of our common sense, our "only," "unquestionable," and "inherently rightful" shared understanding of the issue.

**E.W.** This is, obviously, problematic because *alternative* perspectives of the issue at hand are not just momentarily ignored but, moreover, not cognitively maintained and strengthened as part of our conceptual apparatus.

**G.L.** Exactly. And this is part of the power of metaphor in political language and reasoning. The metaphors that dominate a discourse will greatly determine how both the speaker and the listener think, and what they do *not* think, which is anything that the prevalent metaphoric mapping hides due to the nature of its source domain.

**E.W.** That sounds a tad unnerving. Couldn't people decide to reject the metaphors that public discourse offers them and choose to think about issues in terms of alternative mappings, ones that highlight whatever aspects of a situation are important to *them*?

**G.L.** Theoretically, yes. To a certain degree, political actors and parties can indeed be masters of their own fate when it comes to metaphor and politics. Language and discourses can be analyzed for predominant metaphoric mappings and their effects on our perception of the issue at hand, whether it is taxation, welfare, or the environment. Metaphors that seem to contradict one's understanding of an issue can be disregarded, while metaphors that are in line with one's

---

[18]   See, e.g., Caporale & Dan 2008; Hebb 1949; Shatz 1992.

ideas can be given priority in one's communication. And so on.

But our readers shouldn't get too excited at this prospect. Because the reality is that people very commonly do *not* do any such thing, whether they are involved in social and political action or "merely" citizens in a democratic society. People do *not* question the metaphoric structures that public debates and policy decisions are rooted in — usually they don't even know that they are speaking, thinking, and acting in terms of metaphors.

**E.W.** Because many people, entire nations even, hold outdated beliefs about human reason. People say to themselves, "I know what I think, and I perceive things as they objectively exist in this world. And not only that, I can also *talk* about them as they exist, in a literal sense, without any such thing as metaphor."

**G.L.** And you know what? This is exactly why metaphoric language is so effective — and potentially dangerous — in political public debate.

**E.W.** Because metaphors can create political realities in our minds and we don't even notice it.

**G.L.** And this is not least due to the fact that we are oblivious to the workings of our own reasoning.

Chapter 2

# *How to Parent a Nation*

## The Role of Idealized Family Models for Politics

### 2.1. *Dirty* Thoughts and *Low* Blows:
### Metaphors and morality

**E.W.** The division between conservatives and liberals in America is more than just a discrepancy in material self-interests. It is a battle over values, a moral division. But "morality" itself is quite an abstract idea — we can't touch, see, smell, or taste the thing that is "morality." Ergo, we reason about it in terms of metaphor.

**G.L.** And we know about a dozen or so very basic metaphors for morality. The unique thing about them is that people around the world share them. We all use the same simple metaphors for morality because they stem from very basic, culture-independent human experiences.

This does not imply, by the way, that people use these metaphors equally as much or apply them to the same domains of life. People, and whole societies, can give preference to certain morality metaphors over others.

**E.W.** So we have an extensive metaphor system for morality. We all learn that system as we grow up, because our metaphoric construals of morality are rooted in our basic, culture-independent experiences with well-being—that is, experiences that relate to feeling "good" or being "well off."

We already discussed the Moral Accounting metaphor, which is based on our experience that people are better off in life if they have the things they need. But beyond that, there is a whole series of other experiences that relate to our well-being.

**G.L.** Yes. For instance, we learn that we are better off if we are physically strong and that we are worse off if we are physically weak. That is the basis for the *Morality Is Strength* metaphor, which makes us speak of *weak* performances and *strong* character.

We also learn as a child that we are better off if we can stand up than if we are crawling on the ground. So we learn the metaphor *Morality Is Up*, and say things like, "That was a *low* thing to do," or "I trust him, he's an *upright* person."

We experience that we are better off when we are healthy and worse off when we are sick. So we develop the mapping *Morality Is Health*, and speak of a *healthy* work attitude and people's *sick* or *diseased* minds. We also speak of the *spreading* of bad behavior, which can be *infectious*, amongst a group of children at a birthday party.

Then there's a metaphor that construes morality as walking along a straight path with geographical boundaries. We use this metaphor when we say that someone has *wandered off* the right *path*. We use it when we say that something was a grave *misstep*. And we use it when we accuse someone of *crossing* a *line*.

**E.W.** Another important metaphor for morality is *Morality Is Purity*. As a child, we experience that we are better off when we are clean and worse off when we are not clean. If you have dirty hands from playing outside and you rub your eyes with them, your eyes might itch and burn. You experience that physical impurity has a negative effect on your well-being, and that if you want to feel good, you should avoid impurity.

**G.L.** Based on this metaphoric mapping, we say things like, "He has a *clean* conscience," "I wish I could start over with a *clean* slate," and "He's having *dirty* thoughts."

**E.W.** And Pontius Pilate reportedly washed his hands after his verdict against Jesus. By the way, researchers at the University of Toronto published an interesting study[19] in relation to this. First, they had participants recall moral misdeeds, such as lying to a friend or cheating on an exam. Then, half of the subjects washed their hands, while the other half did *not* get to physically cleanse themselves. What happened next is astonishing: subjects that had washed their hands felt *less* guilty! They literally had a *cleaner* conscience.

**G.L.** This is a great example of how the *Morality Is Purity* metaphor structures not only our language, but also our thoughts, beliefs, and — ultimately — actions.

**E.W.** Let's talk about how metaphors for morality factor into people's political judgment and their conservative or liberal policy stances.

**G.L.** Well, let's take the Moral Accounting metaphor, which we discussed to great length. That metaphor can directly impact people's policy stances on a whole range of issues. Take crime policy in the United States. Our political approaches to crime are firmly rooted in a metaphoric moral accounting system.

The death penalty, for instance, comes out of the notion of moral retribution: if you took someone's life, then the government can take your life in return as a means of *balancing the books*. Murderers *pay* for their actions with something as *valuable* as what they took from others. This is the only way to settle the *debt* that murderers bring upon themselves — retribution.

---

[19]   Zhong & Liljenquist 2006.

**E.W.** Conservatives tend to reason in terms of moral retribution, and conservative crime policy tends to rely on that metaphoric construct.

**G.L.** No doubt about it. But notice that the Moral Accounting metaphor can also bring about the notion of moral restitution, which tends to result in policymaking that focuses on rehabilitation and social reintegration. Progressives tend to endorse the notion of moral restitution when it comes to crime policy.

**E.W.** So that's an example of how moral metaphors factor into conservative and progressive policies. But at a deeper level, how does metaphor explain the schism between the left-leaning and right-leaning camps in the United States, the abysmal split between the conservative and progressive worldviews?

**G.L.** Well, let's talk about another metaphor that is extremely relevant in this context. This metaphor is vital to our moral reasoning about politics. It can determine our beliefs about what's right and what's wrong in politics, our notion of what constitutes good and bad governance. It has to do with family life. Conceptually speaking, political morals are family morals more often than not.

### 2.2. Founding *Fathers* and *Home*land: How we conceptualize nationhood

**E.W.** Why turn to family morals as a conceptual source for political judgment? It seems more logical to assume that morality is derived directly from social norms and institutionalized values in the form of laws.

**G.L.** Recall that our primary experiences in life bring about powerful metaphoric mappings in our minds.

Where did we gain your first experiences with being told what is right and what is wrong? When did we first encounter a moral authority whose job it was to "govern" our life in some way or another, where that authority made decisions on the "right" way to rule over us? Well, as a child in our family. Our parents held authority over us, had to set rules, and teach us right from wrong.

**E.W.** So family is our primary experience with being governed. It constitutes our first experience with being a member of a group that has hierarchical structures. In a family, parents are the legitimate, governing authority. Their method of *parenting* is their way of *governing* your life and that of your siblings.

**G.L.** But not all parents resort to the same ideals and moral beliefs in their parenting strategies. There is no one universal model of parenting — there are *different* models of parenting. Some people believe that parental strictness trumps everything, while others maintain that empathy and mutual respect is the best recipe for raising a good person.

　　Imagine, for instance, that you as a child misbehave. Let's say you sneak a cookie from the cookie jar, knowing that you were supposed to ask your parents first. As your parents see you — with cookie crumbs all over your shirt and chocolate chips on your face — what do they do? Do they immediately punish you with no questions asked, or do they talk to you about the problem with eating too many cookies. Some parents endorse a system of swift punishment. Others prefer a system of dialog and empathy. Families implement different systems of governance.

**E.W.** So the family domain is our primary experience with being governed, and this is why our minds turn to it as an automatic template for reasoning about governance in larger social groups. We automatically map our beliefs about what constitutes ideal family life and parenting onto politics. Whatever we might think is "the right way to run a family" becomes "the right way to run the nation."

**G.L.** Yes, the things we know and think about families serve as a natural conduit for reasoning about the "nation family."

The *Nation As Family* metaphor is so common[20] that we don't even notice it anymore. You might come across it a hundred times while reading the *New York Times* at the breakfast table, and your mind will automatically process the mapping without your even giving it a second thought.

We reason about nations as families all the time. We speak of the founding *fathers* of the United States. The Germans have a *father*land. There's *mother* Russia and *mother* India. Nations send their *sons* and *daughters* to war. And so on. You see, no one questions the notion of founding *fathers* as the right way to speak and reason about the people who founded the American nation.

**E.W.** We talk about the nation in terms of a family and we reason about the nation in terms of a family. And therefore, we map our beliefs about ideal family life onto politics.[21]

**G.L.** Yes, and this mechanism can help us understand the conservative-progressive divide in the United States. I noticed this for the first time in 1994. In 1994, Bill Clinton was president, and we were about to have congressional elections. In the dawn of that election, six weeks before Election Day, the Republicans published a document called the "Contract With America", and they won the elections that year.

**E.W.** The "Contract With America" simply laid out the Republicans' positions on a whole range of domestic and foreign policy issues. There was nothing outstanding about it.

**G.L.** But there was. I remember the day that document was published as if it were yesterday. I sat in my office, hunched over my desk with a cup of coffee, and carefully read through the whole document, paragraph by paragraph. And when I had read through the whole thing, I realized that I

---

[20]   See, e.g., Cienki 2005; Lakoff 1996; Musolff 2004, 2006; Schlesinger & Lau 2000.

[21]   Lakoff 1996; Wehling 2013; Feinberg et al. 2016; Wehling et al. 2015.

didn't understand any of it. I sat there scratching my head, wondering what I was missing.

You see, the purpose of the document was to proclaim to voters what the Republican party believed, what the party stood for, and what type of governance people could expect if they casted their votes for the conservatives.

**E.W.** And so?

**G.L.** Well, the document outlined the Republicans' political platform, which included support for a flat tax and opposition to abortion. And I asked myself, "What do taxes and abortion have to do with each other?" The document also declared the Republicans' opposition to environmental regulation, and I wondered, "What on earth does environmental regulation have to do with a flat tax and bans on abortion?" In the document the Republicans also expressed their belief that every American citizen should be allowed to own and use guns. And I asked, "What in heaven does the right to bear arms have to do with being for a flat tax, against environmental protection, and against abortion?"

I just couldn't make sense of the political statement being made by the document as a whole. Sure, I fully understood each of the policy stances being taken — there was nothing new there. But what I couldn't wrap my head around was how all those positions hung together. How did they come together to constitute a Republican identity and the promise of Republican governance?

I was about to leave things at telling myself that Republicans were quite interesting folks. Curiously, they seemed to have no coherence of any sort across their political stances — Lord only knew how they came up with such a diverse set of them.

And then it hit me — I also didn't know what it was that held together *my own* progressive positions on issues such as guns, the environment, abortion, and taxation. Never mind the Republicans! I couldn't put my finger on what it was that lent coherence to *my* positions!

**E.W.** So in essence you didn't understand what differentiated you from a conservative on a level that was somehow *deeper* and more *meaningful* than just the fact that you held a set of contradictory issue positions.

**G.L.** Yes. And I realized that the question I was posing was one that needed to be tackled in cognitive science, because it was a question about human reasoning—in this case, conservative and progressive reasoning. So I embarked on a quest to find out what conceptual patterns gave rise to political conservatism and progressivism.

**E.W.** You could have saved yourself a lot of time by consulting a political dictionary, where you would have read something along the lines of: conservatism has its linguistic roots in the Latin "conservare," which translates to *keeping intact, preserving,* or *maintaining.* Political conservatism is based on the idea of safeguarding traditional values and societal norms. Progressivism, in contrast, is conceptually rooted in a positive attitude towards societal progress and change.

**G.L.** The problem is that this vague definition is as prevalent as it is defective. But let's put it to the test. Conservatives are supposed to maintain traditional values and norms. But minimal taxation is not a traditional American value. Nor is military aggression against other countries a traditional American value. And torturing people is not a traditional American value, either. On the other hand, progressives are supposed to push for change and oppose traditional values, but putting taxes towards the common wealth is a traditional American value, as is sharing responsibility for building and maintaining public infrastructure. And so on.

**E.W.** So you discarded one of the most common theories about conservative and progressive politics to see whether we can make sense of the two political camps in terms of what we now know about human cognition and conceptual models.

**G.L.** Yes, and I didn't get anywhere for months, until finally something caught my attention. Family values. Conservatives constantly talked about them. Family values this and family values that. I thought, "Why do politicians that face issues such as global warming, nuclear armament, and social disparity talk endlessly about family values? Why would *anyone* spend so much time—and substantial amounts of money—campaigning for family values?"

Then I remembered a term paper one of my students had written on how people speak metaphorically about the nation as a family.

**E.W.** And suddenly, the conservative obsession with talking about family values seemed anything but nonsensical.

**G.L.** Exactly. In fact, it seemed quite the opposite of nonsensical. It seemed like conservatives were onto something that progressives had not even begun to understand, much less implement in their communication.

### 2.3. As You Deal with Children, So with Citizens You Shall Deal: Parenting and politics

**E.W.** And so you figured if there are two different moral worldviews in politics—conservative and progressive—then there are probably two conflicting family and parenting models at their foundations.

**G.L.** Indeed. And I was still in the midst of trying to figure out what family ideals play a role in the formation of the two worldviews when a friend contacted me. She was a Political Science professor here at UC, Berkeley, and the *National Science Foundation* had approached her with a plea. They needed her to compose a survey item that would allow researchers to detect whether someone was conservative or progressive. She was to find one single question, the answer to which would give away a person's political identity. She was asking all her friends what they thought that question should be. I didn't really have an answer. So I started asking all my friends the same question. Coincidentally, my friend

Paul Baum was in town that week, and so I asked him, too. Paul was wise, and he was a psychotherapist, and he knew a lot about people. He looked at me and said, "George, I know the perfect question to ask."

**E.W.** A single item measure for political identity — one question that would be a dead giveaway as to whether someone was politically conservative or progressive?

**G.L.** Yes. The question Paul proposed was this: "When your baby cries at night, do you pick him up?" I said, "Why? What's behind this, Paul?" And he, being the therapist he was, said, "Think about it, George."

So I started to think about what kind of parenting ideals would elicit different replies to the question: "When your baby cries at night, do you pick him up?" I looked at the mechanisms, elements, and inferences of the *Nation As Family* metaphor in detail, and I started bringing them together with parenting ideals and all the conservative and progressive policy stances.

In the end, I arrived at two models that accounted for this data triangle: the Strict Father and the Nurturant Parent family.[22]

**E.W.** General affinities between governmental strictness and conservatism as well as governmental nurturance and progressivism have been previously observed, across academic disciplines and throughout history. One could say that what you're saying isn't exactly breaking news.

**G.L.** No doubt, those tendencies have been talked and written about. That's not the point. We all know that conservative policy tends to be "more strict" on criminals, and that progressive policy tends to be "more kind" towards the socially disadvantaged. But, first of all, the details of the two family models as they relate to conservative and progressive moral reasoning and, ultimately, policy go far beyond a mere distinction of acting in a generally "strict" or

---

[22]   Lakoff 1996.

"nurturant" manner. The two models are highly complex, with many interconnected subareas of moral beliefs.[23] Keeping that point in mind is crucial to avoid oversimplifying the conservative and progressive worldviews.

**E.W.** What's more, we ought to ask ourselves how the differences in moral cognition between conservatives and progressives come about and why they prove to be more or less stable across societies and over time.

**G.L.** Right. And to understand all these issues, we need to understand how conservatism and progressivism are anchored in our conceptual systems, and how they relate to our everyday, unconscious reasoning.

---

23   Lakoff 1996, 2004; Wehling 2013; Wehling et al. 2015.

# Chapter 3

# Moral Politics Theory
## The Strict Father and Nurturant Parent Models

### 3.1. Governing with a Firm Hand:
### The Strict Father model and conservatism

**E.W.** Moral Politics Theory holds that individuals' political stances stem from deeply held moral beliefs that are conceptually anchored in parenting models. Conservatives endorse a Strict Father model, while progressives endorse a Nurturant Parent model.

Let's talk about the Strict Father model first. In this model, the father is the head of the family. He is the legitimate authority and his authority is not to be challenged. The family needs such a moral authority because the world is a dangerous place, and the job of a father is to protect the family against evil.

Ergo, the model holds a classic good–evil dichotomy that divides the world into the "good guys" and the "bad guys."

**G.L.** Exactly. According to the Strict Father model, there is good and bad in the world. The father, as the legitimate authority of the family, knows right from wrong, and he is naturally good and morally upright. He defends the family against evil, and he teaches his children to develop moral strength. The mother cannot do the job of the father, because women are seen as less strong. The duty of the mother is to support her husband in his authority. This model has gender-based parental roles.

Moreover, the world is assumed to be innately competitive. It is the father's responsibility to compete successfully in the world so he can take care of his family. He must also teach his children how to compete with others so that they can become successful and self-reliant when they grow up. So the world is both dangerous and competitive.

**E.W.** Another important notion about the world is that in it there are absolute rights and wrongs: people's behaviors, actions, and beliefs are either right—or they are wrong. The father, as the legitimate authority in the family, knows right from wrong. So, since "Father knows best," he teaches the children right from wrong and he communicates this to the children in a hierarchical way. He sets strict rules and requests absolute obedience. That's it. No discussion.

**G.L.** Yes, and obedience to the father as the legitimate moral authority in the family is seen as moral behavior in children. It is a value in itself. And it is upheld through a system of reward and punishment. This means, quite simply, that bad behavior in children is always punished and good behavior is rewarded. Punishment is seen as absolutely crucial. It is the parents' moral duty to punish bad behavior in children, because they assume this is the only way they will develop discipline and strength. And since children are born "bad," they will learn how to be good only through punishment.

**E.W.** What does that mean—children are born "*bad*"?

**G.L.** It means they are born undisciplined. They want to do whatever feels good to them. They tend to want to indulge themselves. So they need to learn right from wrong. Self-indulgence, for instance, is categorically wrong. Self-discipline, on the other hand, is inherently right. Children don't know this when they are born, and parents must teach them about it by rewarding what is good behavior and punishing bad behavior. Punishment is the more important concept, though. It is through punishment that children learn strength and self-discipline.

**E.W.** Are you saying that the need to punish wins over parental love in the Strict Father model?

**G.L.** No. Parents who believe in this model love their children just as much as any other parents. Punishment is viewed not as a lack of love but as a sign of love — "tough love." It is seen as the parents' moral duty to punish their children. Even if it hurts them to do so, even if it is a matter of, "It hurts me more than it hurts you." Parents who don't punish their children, who fail to teach them that wrong behaviors result in painful "consequences," are regarded as immoral and irresponsible.

**E.W.** From the viewpoint of the Strict Father model, parents who do not punish have failed as parents.

**G.L.** Because punishment helps children become self-disciplined and morally strong. Think of it this way: if you are punished often enough by a moral authority, you will learn to discipline yourself, to be your own moral authority! Once that point is reached, you are your own authority — you can follow your self-interests and compete successfully in the world rather than being dependent on others.

**E.W.** It sounds to me like we just came full circle. Psychologically speaking, the concept of self-discipline feeds off of a good–evil dichotomy: self-disciplined people are able to overcome their own inner evil, that "immoral" fragment within themselves that needs disciplining.

**G.L.** I agree. There are two ways of dividing the world up into good and bad. There is the external "good" and "bad," which is out there in the world. And there is internal "good" and "bad" within us. Once you have developed *moral strength,* you can fight both internal and external forms of evil. You can fight evil in the world — through warfare, for instance—and you can fight the evil within you—through "self-discipline."

**E.W.** The notion of reward and punishment is central to the Strict Father model. Let's talk about how it affects conservative domestic policy.

**G.L.** First of all, conservatives in the US are working under the assumption that everyone can be successful. No matter what your background might be, if you build up enough moral strength and self-discipline, then you can make it. This is referred to as, "Pulling yourself up by the bootstraps."

**E.W.** So under this model, anyone who is self-disciplined can be successful. And people's social and economic success, in turn, is proof of their moral strength. And there's a converse argument hidden in this equation, something that is automatically implied: people who are not successful are lacking in moral strength and self-discipline. They are morally weak. And people who are morally weak are bad people who deserve their poverty.

Within this conceptual model, being poor is a natural and warranted punishment for people's moral weakness!

**G.L.** Yes, and the worst thing you could do to those people would be to step in and give them things they have not earned for themselves! Why? Because giving people things they haven't earned means to rob them of their chance to grow strong—how are they to *ever* learn self-discipline if you do not let them "sink or swim." Making their lives easier would mean to actively harm them. This is why conservatives in the US are less than fond of social welfare. It's not that conservatives simply don't care about whether or not someone receives social welfare. They are generally against the idea of welfare. They think it's a bad idea to give economically unsuccessful people things that make their lives easier.

**E.W.** So in the eyes of conservatives, welfare is a form of governmental indulgence, which makes citizens weak and dependent, and thus constitutes immoral governance. And, by this reasoning, "do-gooders" do a whole lot of bad.

**G.L.** Yes, they do, in more ways than one. "Do-gooders" are bad because they make their fellow citizens weak and dependent by stealing their opportunity to grow strong and self-disciplined. Additionally, "do-gooders" fail to pursue their *own* self-interest, which means that don't play by the rules of competition, so they hurt the system that makes people good and might depend on others one day themselves.

**E.W.** Welfare interferes with the only societal apparatus that can produce "good" people, meaning people with loads of self-discipline and their self-interests as their top priority?

**G.L.** That's the idea, yes. Welfare turns the system of reward and punishment belly up. This, in turn, damages society as a whole because it takes away people's incentive to seek their self-interests and become self-disciplined. The only moral way of running a society—and governing a nation—is to implement and uphold a system of social and economic rivalry.

**E.W.** In short, a *moral* society needs as much competition as it can get.

**G.L.** And for this to be accomplished, there have to be in place significant rewards for the disciplined and severe repercussions for the weak. By the way, this type of moral reasoning also motivates the conservative positions on taxation. High taxes are an immoral punishment of people who have done the right thing—develop discipline and thereby become successful. Many folks believe that the conservative positions on taxes merely have to do with making money for the rich: the rich and influential want to preserve their wealth, thus they favor low taxation. But that is not true. Or at the very least, it is not the whole story. Conservatives oppose taxes because they are a form of immoral governance. They punish the good guys. That's morally outrageous to poor conservatives just as much as to rich ones.

### 3.2. The Strongest Might Not Survive: The misinterpretation of Darwin

**E.W.** Conservatives got it right then, some might say. They understand the basic principles of Social Darwinism: competition helps society achieve its full potential because it allows the strongest group members to rise to the top.

**G.L.** Social Darwinism is a myth. It's a distortion of Charles Darwin's ideas and writings. You see, Darwin came from England. During his times, his country was under the thumb of the conservative Church of England. In short, England was under the influence of a church that endorsed Strict Father ideals. So when Darwin was working out his theories and made them public, church folks said, "Hah, didn't we know it all along! People who survive and thrive in society *deserve* to be on top, because nature intends for the strongest to be on top. In fact, we must leave people to their own fate, so that the strong will survive and society is sieved of the weak."

Well, Darwin said no such thing. So where did Social Darwinism fall off the track?

**E.W.** Well, for one, Social Darwinism is built on the notion that societies function just like natural environments—humans in a society are like fish in a pond or insects in a tree. But human societies are not "natural environments" in this sense. They are construed by humans. So entirely equating the two domains is problematic. It conceals the fact that the societies we live in were substantially molded over time by human decision-making—decisions on the distribution of resources, norms, laws, and so on. Any theories that equate the two domains all too lightheartedly should raise some eyebrows.

**G.L.** Yes, that's doubtlessly true. But there's another issue with Social Darwinism. The dilemma with Social Darwinism is that it distorted the claims Darwin made about nature. Darwin was reporting on the "survival of the *fittest*," not the "survival of the *strongest*." He did not say that *strong* animals survive. He said that the animals that survive are those that *fit* the best in any given ecological niche.

Let's assume you are a green butterfly and I am a purple butterfly. We live in the same jungle. We are neighbors so to say. We eat from the same food sources and we face the same predators. Let's now assume that this jungle is full of green leaves, and that purple leaves are not as common.

**E.W.** That puts me at an advantage, because predators will not easily spot me amongst all those green leaves. But you, well, that's a different story. You're quite an eye catcher.

**G.L.** I got the short end of the stick. Your chance of *survival* is better, because you *fit* better. The same goes for your off-spring, if they are lucky enough to inherit your green wings. They will also *fit* well into the ecological niche. This is what Darwin meant by "survival of the fittest."

**E.W.** Darwin would say the reason I survived the jungle is not that I was stronger than you. I just happened to be greener than you.

**G.L.** Exactly. Survival does not necessarily favor individual strength. It varies based on attributes of the ecological niche you find yourself in—and the question of whether or not your characteristics fit those attributes well enough to survive and thrive.

But when Darwin returned to England and laid out his findings, members of the English church interpreted his ideas in terms of Strict Father values and metaphorically applied them to society.

**E.W.** They believed that they had found proof for the notion that people needed to seek their self-interests and be left to sink or swim, and that only the strongest should thrive.

**G.L.** Yes. They had found a way to frame their moral theory about humans and societies as a scientific theory. They used Darwin's findings to back up their beliefs about moral social selection.

By the way, Charles Darwin fought against this interpretation of his theories. He objected to the notion of a natural "social selection."

### 3.3. By the Hand of Adam Smith:
### Moral markets

**E.W.** Isn't it astounding just how effortlessly the notion of Social Darwinism goes hand in hand with the notion of an unrestricted "free market," that is, a maximally competitive market with minimal governmental intervention that allows for the "strongest" to economically, well, survive?

**G.L.** Indeed. And the notion of Social Darwinism is frequently used to argue for the necessity of unrestricted "free markets." But there's a problem with this idea — there is actually no such thing as "free" markets. All markets are controlled by someone. All markets have rules and regulations. Usually, those regulations are to the advantage of some and the disadvantage of others.

**E.W.** Nonetheless, there is a myth of the market as a *natural force*.

**G.L.** That notion stems from Adam Smith, who claimed that if everyone were to follow their own interests and maximize their economic well-being, then everyone's well-being would be maximized through the *invisible hand* — a natural regulating force inherent to market economies.

**E.W.** This has become a conservative credo, a moral narrative: it is moral to maximize your self-interests in an unrestricted and highly competitive market.

**G.L.** Yes. But, again, there is no such thing as a "free" market. That's a folktale. All markets are man-made. All

markets have rules. The stock market has rules, and someone made those rules. The "World Trade Organization" has
trade regulations that fill more than 900 pages. Market rules
are not made by nature or an invisible hand of any sort.
They are created and maintained by people. And they can be
changed at any time — by people.

Maybe it's time for progressives to publicly discuss the
fact that the *free market* is a myth, that market rules have been
created and can be changed, and that the rules are to the
advantage of some and disadvantage of others. You see, as
long as progressives stick with the conservative metaphor of
a *free market*, they themselves always end up being perceived
as the people who seek to make the market somehow "less
free" when they call for changes in rules and regulations.

### 3.4. Governing with an Empathic Eye: The Nurturant Parent model and progressivism

**E.W.** So progressives make a huge mistake by using the
conservative *free market* metaphor because it follows Strict
Father morality. Maybe it's time to discuss the family model
that governs progressive politics, namely, the Nurturant
Parent model.

**G.L.** The Nurturant Parent model starts with the notion that
it's moral to show empathy, to nurture, and to take on individual as well as social responsibility.

In the Nurturant Parent family, parents strive to raise
their children to become nurturers through guiding by
example, through being nurturant towards them. One way
of doing that is to empower one's children to follow their
dreams, whatever those might be.

Cooperation with others is seen as more important than
competition. Parents teach their children to empathize with
others, and to be able to see the world through other
people's eyes. And they teach them to cooperate with others,
and to take on responsibility not just for themselves but also
the community around them.

To teach children empathy, parents lead by example,
showing a high degree of empathy for their children. They

seek to understand their children's viewpoints, and they speak to them in an open and respectful manner.

**E.W.** So instead of hierarchical communication, the Nurturant Parent model focuses on open communication at eye level. Children are encouraged to speak their minds and develop their own ideas, and there is mutual respect between children and parents. This is different from other parenting models, in which children are expected to show respect for their parents, but not vice versa.

**G.L.** Yes, however, in the Nurturant Parent model it is still true that parents are the family authority, and they are the ones who ultimately make the decisions. But decisions are discussed with children. So there is a notion of account-ability towards the children, and openness and dialog about why certain rules are set and certain decisions made.

**E.W.** So how do children learn to respect their parents' authority if not through the threat of punishment?

**G.L.** They learn through the love and respect that children feel for their parents based on the ways in which their parents interact with them. Instead of obedience to strict rules and repercussions for rule breaking, this model focuses on positive attachment. Children want to do well and follow their parents' guidance because they want to make their parents proud and happy, and because they trust their parents to watch out for their well-being and respect them.

**E.W.** What else?

**G.L.** Well, children are taught to strive for personal excellence: their parents empower them to follow their dreams and so they seek to do well in the world and for themselves. The crucial thing is that success is not under-stood as "success over others" or "winning against others," but as fulfilling one's own potential. For instance, personal success can mean to have helped someone else, or to have taken on responsibility for a group of people with no prospect of any kind of material reward.

**E.W.** You know, that almost sounds as if the difference between the Strict Father and Nurturant Parent models can be reduced to egoism and altruism.

**G.L.** No, the models are not about egoism versus altruism. The Strict Father model sees the pursuit of self-interest over other people's interests as moral behavior. This is not seen as egoism at all. In a way, it is seen as pro-social behavior. Because this model works under the premises that if everyone maximizes their own well-being at any cost, everyone's well-being is maximized. Watching out for yourself is acting in a socially responsible way because no one will have to look out for you, and because you thereby keep the system thriving that helps people grow strong so they can take care of themselves. If everyone follows this template, then everyone will be fine.

**E.W.** And by this logic, looking after yourself is the best way to watch out for others.

**G.L.** Exactly. And as for the Nurturant Parent model, the goal is not to raise children to be completely altruistic. In fact, full-blown altruism would get in the way of children learning social responsibility. Why? Because individual and social responsibility go hand in hand. Let's think for a moment about what it means to be *truly* responsible. Well, any real responsibility starts with responsibility for oneself because you can only care for others if you take good care of yourself.

**E.W.** So both the Strict Father and Nurturant Parent models incorporate the notion of individual responsibility. But in progressivism, individual responsibility is seen as a basis for social responsibility, and not as a means to be maximally independent of others.

**G.L.** Right. The Nurturant Parent model sees moral value in striving for your goals and self-fulfillment, being happy and healthy, and nurturing yourself—all those aspects of self-care enable you to care for others. In this model, parents raise their children to become caregivers for themselves and others. Obviously, this is quite different from the conventional notion of altruism, which implies putting the needs of others before your own needs and desires at all costs.

**E.W.** And yet, the Nurturant Parent model has an easily discernible weak spot, namely, a lack of discipline. Children are raised in a *"laissez-faire"* manner, doing whatever they please, with no strict rules and no moral authority.

**G.L.** No. The Nurturant Parent model does not imply *laissez-faire* parenting, in which parents are relatively uninvolved in their children's lives and let them do whatever they please. Actually, it's quite the opposite. Raising children to become individually and socially responsible takes a tremendous amount of effort and involvement with the child, and it requires commitment to constantly model the desired moral behavior for the child.

However, your critique is an interesting one, because it reveals a fundamental misinterpretation of progressive family values by conservatives. Conservatives commonly understand nurturant parenting as *indulgent* or *laissez-faire* parenting.

**E.W.** *Indulgent* parenting means to give children anything they want without requiring them to learn self-responsibility. *Laissez-faire* parenting means to let children do whatever they want without setting boundaries.

**G.L.** And so in *indulgent* and *laissez-faire* parenting, children are not required to take responsibility for themselves and others. This is the opposite of nurturant parenting. Conservatives commonly don't see any difference between those three models because none of them is based on the notion of a strict moral authority, absolute right and wrong, punishment, and obedience.

**E.W.** But how can the Nurturant Parent model be understood as a value-based model, a model of morality, if there are no clear rules that tell the children what is right and what is wrong?

**G.L.** Of course there are notions of "right" and "wrong" inherent in the model. But they are less intricate than those in the Strict Father model. They reside at a higher, more general level of behavior. "Moral" and "immoral" actions manifest themselves in how people generally interact with others. For instance, it's wrong to harm other people or allow them to be harmed by others. It's right to understand people, see them for who they are, recognize their individual needs and care for them. Those are the essential moral principles of the Nurturant Parent model.

**E.W.** In order to implement such general principles in everyday life, one would need a lot of empathy. It's empathy that enables us to understand what constitutes "harming" and "caring" in any given social context. One has to be able to walk in other people's shoes, to understand their needs and struggles.

**G.L.** Yes. And so in a way you might be right—this model doesn't have a collection of clearly defined "right" and "wrong" behaviors. Also, moral and immoral behavior is not rooted in a categorical division of the world into "good" and "evil," where some actions make you good and others make you evil, no matter what the context. Moral behavior in the nurturant worldview requires empathy toward people and their situations. In the Nurturant Parent family, children are brought up to understand others and empathize with them, not to be obedient to an authority that dictates right and wrong.

**E.W.** So we are looking at progressive moral tolerance instead of conservative moral doctrine?

**G.L.** Well, yes, in order to understand others, you first need to tolerate them. You have to be willing and able to consider their perspective on things. Rather than *judging* people, you must strive to *comprehend* them. Those are two very different modes of operating.

**E.W.** And if your ultimate goal is to comprehend others, to see their perspective on things, then you cannot maintain a system that divides the world into right and wrong based on values that are highly specific to your own moral system. That would, in fact, be quite problematic, and it would make you prone to push your values onto others.

**G.L.** Yes. But something else comes into play here, and it has to do with the notion of absolute moral authority in the Strict Father model and the idea that the world is divided into good and evil. In the Strict Father family, the father is an absolute moral authority that is not to be challenged — neither from within the family nor from outside the family. And since the father is the legitimate authority in the family, the values he holds are by definition "good" and "right." So how does he view people who live by values that differ from his?

Well, those people and their beliefs threaten the legitimate authority of the father, who is supposed to know right from wrong.

**E.W.** Ergo, they cannot be tolerated.

**G.L.** Exactly. And so it becomes the moral duty of the father to not just uphold his values within the family, but to also defend them against other value systems. Let me give you a perfect example of how this works in the US. Take a conservative family father who lives in a small village somewhere in Kansas. Let's call him Joe. Why should Joe be against gay marriage in California? Why should he care *at all* whether two men in love get married in San Francisco? He's probably not planning to move from Kansas to San Francisco any time soon, either. And the chances of two openly gay, married men from San Francisco wanting to relocate to Kansas are slim. Therefore, the conservative family father Joe would be highly unlikely to ever even meet the happily married gay couple! So why should it *matter* to Joe whether or not gay people who live thousands of miles away get married to each other? Well, it matters to Joe because the notion of a non-gendered family threatens the value system by which he runs his family. The idea that families could have *two* fathers or, in the case of married women, *no* father, threatens Joe's moral authority in a gender-based authority system.

**E.W.** So tolerating values that oppose Strict Father morality is seen as moral weakness, as lacking a moral backbone. In contrast, a progressive doesn't think of tolerance as a sign of weakness. In the Nurturant Parent model, tolerance is a sign of strength—it is based on empathy, and it allows for people to cooperate with and watch out for each other. And not only that, tolerance is also necessary in order to take on responsibility for others.

**G.L.** Yes, because taking on social responsibility means to strive to elevate everyone's well-being. And people's well-being is maximized if they are allowed to be who they are, and to strive for individual self-fulfillment. So in this model, instead of having rigid notions of what constitutes the "right" and "wrong" ways of being, people must be allowed to be who they are, as individuals. This means that you welcome different religions, different sexual and gender identities, different cultural norms, and so on because they are not perceived as a threat to the progressive value system. In fact, *not* tolerating those who are different from us would constitute a threat to the progressive value system, because that would violate its core values—empathy, nurturance, and social responsibility.

**E.W.** But there *are* baddies in the world! So even progressive tolerance must end somewhere, or else you become guilty of turning a blind eye on injustice.

**G.L.** Yes, progressive tolerance has a natural boundary. And that boundary is harm. Progressive tolerance ends where harm to others begins. Protecting others against harm is an important component of the Nurturant Parent model.

**E.W.** Hold on. Just a minute ago we said that defending one's family against evil is a Strict Father idea. Have we just uncovered a moral parallel between the two worldviews?

**G.L.** Not quite. There's a difference between "defending" one's family in terms of a Strict Father worldview and "protecting" one's family in terms of a Nurturant Parent worldview. The strict father defends his family. Think of the conservative Gun Lobby. Why should conservatives be in favor of gun ownership? What type of worldview would lead someone to favor policies that equip citizens with firearms? The answer is, one that assumes that this world is a dangerous place and that there are evil people out there. In order to protect your family against evil you might have to shoot evil people, because sometimes you need to "fight evil with evil tools." In the Strict Father model it is morally right to use guns as weapons for "defending" one's family.

Now, let's look at the Nurturant Parent model and the notion of protecting people against harm. If protection from harm is one of your moral duties, then you need to make sure that citizens harm one another as little as possible. However, the legalization of firearms in the US makes it very easy for people to injure and even kill each other! That's why people who operate by the progressive worldview advocate for banning guns. You ban guns to protect people from shooting each other. You stop giving them guns, and you take munitions off the supermarket shelves.

**E.W.** So progressive gun policy is based on the notion of protection against harm. There are also other policies that are rooted in this moral principle. Take consumer protection, which strives to protect citizens against having to eat food that contains poisonous substances, resulting in serious long-term health issues. Or take environmental protection, which strives to protect people against having to breathe polluted air and drink polluted water.

**G.L.** Or take sex education, which strives to protect young people from unplanned pregnancies and sexually transmittable diseases. Young people need to be educated on these subjects to be protected and to protect themselves. Conservatives in the US do not share this view. They fight sex education in schools under the presumption that such education will lead to sexual activity among young people.

**E.W.** One striking feature of the US, compared to other Western democracies, is its radical punitive system. Children and teenagers, for instance, can be sentenced to prison. How do the conservative and progressive notions of "protecting one's citizens" influence crime policy in the US?

**G.L.** Our justice system was not always as punitive as it has become today. It changed under the influence of conservatives. According to Strict Father morality, being a criminal is equated with being a bad, immoral person. One task of the justice system is to make sure that this badness—this immorality—doesn't *spread* throughout society. This type of reasoning is based on one of the metaphors we discussed earlier—the *Morality As Health* metaphor. How does one best protect society against immoral contamination? By locking away people who are immoral.

**E.W.** This reasoning is based on the notion of "direct causation," which is a cornerstone of the Strict Father model: people who break the law do so because they are inherently immoral, bad people.

**G.L.** Exactly! And those "bad apples" must be removed from society. Just ponder for a moment the conceptual premises of the conservative "three strikes" law. Under this law, people who break the law three times get a life sentence, regardless of the details of the three crimes.

**E.W.** The Nurturant Parent model infers a different way of reasoning about crime. This model considers the notion of "systemic causation." It assumes that crime is the outcome of a number of distinct but interrelated societal causes.

**G.L.** Voila. And therefore, the most efficient way to fight crime is to fight its root causes via preventative social policies that counter problems such as poverty, racism, lack of education and health care, and so on. Simply put, progressives believe that the best anti-crime policies are those that help to prevent crime before it happens, policies that grant people chances in life and protect them from despair and social aggression. In Nurturant Parent reasoning, protecting society against crime means to counteract its roots, not to prosecute and lock up criminals after the fact.

**E.W.** Moreover, while an ideal Strict Father society would maximize competition with minimal programs that indulge the weak, an ideal Nurturant Parent society would see governmental nurturance as a moral obligation.

**G.L.** Precisely. Government programs are necessary to help people who are in need of help. Social welfare is based on the notions of empathy and empowerment. In any society, there are people who are socially and economically disadvantaged. And there are people who can't take care of themselves, for various reasons. There are people who are physically or psychologically hurt. There are elderly people. There are people who are born with disabilities and are unable to take care of themselves. There are people who have suffered a great deal in their lives for *various* reasons, and they can no longer take care of themselves. So there are a lot of people who aren't doing well, because they have encountered or were born into circumstances that put them at significant social and economic disadvantages.

**E.W.** The Nurturant Parent model has a number of moral principles that stipulate what a moral society must provide. One core principle is that there are limits to how harshly human beings may be treated.

**G.L.** Or, to put it a different way, there are acceptable standards as to how human beings *must* be treated *at* the very *least*. For instance, people may not be allowed to die of hunger, people may not be left to live on the streets, and people should not be left without basic medical care. Every citizen in a society should be granted a minimum standard of human dignity. And it is the moral obligation of the government to see to that.

### 3.5. The Commonwealth Principle:
### Moral taxation

**E.W.** Social infrastructures like the ones you just talked about are kept alive via taxation. Conservatives in the US are in favor of low taxation, and we discussed how this position emerges from Strict Father morality: high taxes are seen as an immoral punishment of self-discipline and a threat to economic competition. What does the Nurturant Parent worldview say about taxation?

**G.L.** The Nurturant Parent model entails that citizens assume responsibility for each other and care for each other, and promotes that the government should enable citizens to do this. This idea is by no means new. Think back to the times when Franklin Roosevelt was President of the US. Roosevelt revived a historic principle of the United States, the "Commonwealth Principle."

**E.W.** It's a simple principle: use the common wealth for the common good. You collectively raise money via taxes and then use those funds to build and maintain an infrastructure that benefits everyone.

**G.L.** And this infrastructure empowers all citizens to follow their dreams and life goals. Well, to this day the US lives by the "Commonwealth Principle" — we collect taxes in order to use the shared wealth for the common good. The public infrastructure we maintain today is vast! It affects the every-day life of every single citizen.

Let me guess. This morning, you probably sat down and had breakfast. And given the times we live in, you probably checked your emails and Facebook while having breakfast. Maybe you read the *New York Times* on your iPad.

**E.W.** Something along those lines, yes.

**G.L.** Well, the internet was developed with tax money. The satellite communication system that allows us to make calls on mobile phones was developed with tax money. Electricity is available in cities as well as in rural areas because we used our tax money to build an electric infrastructure that provides access for everyone, even the folks in rural areas of the Middle West. Our banking system, which keeps banks from collapsing, is financed with tax money, and so is the stock market regulation system, which keeps the stock markets honest. The judicial system is largely funded via tax money, even though about nine tenths of the work this system does is concerned with business and corporate law.

**E.W.** In short, every person that makes a living in the US is using the common wealth. Everyone who runs a business, and anyone who makes tons of money running a business, not only *built* that business using the public infrastructures but also *maintains* that business by using the commonly financed infrastructure.

**G.L.** Yes, you take on a loan with a bank, you sign a contract, you use the communication system, and you drive on streets to get to clients or transport goods. You are able to do all those things because tax money has been used toward building the necessary infrastructures. And the more money you make, the more you probably use those infrastructures —more advertising, more goods transportation, more contracts, more loans, and so on. And so if you use the infrastructure more than others because you run a big business, well, then you should also contribute a fair share in taxes to maintain that infrastructure.

**E.W.** And yet, many business owners in the US firmly believe that they made it on their own, without the help of others. They believe that they are "self-made" businessmen or businesswomen. This means there has to be a conceptual template that stands in contrast to the common wealth idea and simply ignores taxation-based public empowerment.

**G.L.** You are absolutely right. Many people simply do not see that they use the public infrastructure on a daily basis as they go about their lives. Many people don't see that they heavily rely on our shared wealth. The reason lies in the nature of the Strict Father model. If you believe that the world is a competitive place, and that you stand in perpetual competition with those around you, then you see yourself as working *against* others. The ideal strict father figure not only *makes* it in this world, but does so on his or her own. Core values in this model are self-reliance and self-interest, not shared interests and social responsibility.

**E.W.** The strict father does not cooperate with others — he beats others to the prize!

**G.L.** Which is why the notion of a public infrastructure doesn't fit into this model. The ideal strict father has no appreciation of the fact that society has helped him from the very beginning, and that all his endeavors and successes are based on things that the community has built and continuously maintains for everyone. It would mean that individual success is not the product of moral strength and self-discipline, and it would mean that the world is not inescapably competitive.

### 3.6. Idealized Reality:
### Of strict mothers and nurturant fathers

**E.W.** Since 2006, Germany has had a female chancellor, Angela Merkel, who is a member of the German conservative CDU. Margaret Thatcher was a decidedly strict political figure in the UK. Can women be Strict Fathers?

**G.L.** You bet. Women can be metaphoric Strict Fathers of entire nations. And women can take on the ideal-typical role of the strict father in their families. This is often true for single mothers, who believe they need to compensate for the absence of a male authority figure in their family. A woman who believes in the Strict Father model may slap or hit her children when they are disobedient. So yes, women can, more or less effortlessly, assume the role of the strict father in their families, and they can be metaphoric Strict Fathers in politics.

And by the way, there are also families in which spouses hold different worldviews. The father may endorse a Nurturant Parent worldview, while his wife believes in the Strict Father model. This is quite common. Innumerable marriages end because the spouses hold different moral belief systems and cannot agree on how to best run the family and raise their offspring.

**E.W.** One might ask: given the various ways in which the Strict Father and Nurturant Parent models may apply in real life — should we ascribe them relevance at all?

**G.L.** Yes, they are equally as relevant as all Idealized Cognitive Models.[24] They help us reason about the world in a structured way. They are ideal prototypes, and they help us understand, judge, and categorize the world.

The two family models don't have to occur in everyday life in their exact *idealized* form. The *Nation As Family* metaphor and its two moral contestations, Strict Father and Nurturant Parent morality, structure the ways in which we think about moral parenting and moral governance in terms of two clearly distinguishable, idealized models.

**E.W.** But you do not have to grow up in a family that is an ideal version of either model in order to understand them. And there are many families that stray from the idealized versions of a Strict Father or Nurturant Parent family.

**G.L.** And yet, people automatically resort to idealtypical models in their everyday reasoning. It's just how the mind works. Idealized Cognitive Models are central to our everyday cognition.

**E.W.** And if the idealized model we endorse the most is Strict Father morality, then we're likely politically more

---

[24]    Lakoff 1987a, 1987b; Wehling 2013; also see Croft & Cruse 2004, p. 28.

conservative. If we endorse a Nurturant Parent model, we're likely more progressive. All the while, policies that may be "morally wrong" in the eyes of a progressive can be highly moral in the eyes of a conservative—simply put: there's no accounting for moral taste.

**G.L.** Yes, it's as simple as that. In the eyes of a conservative, policies that are in line with Strict Father ideals are highly moral. A progressive may say, "What you do in politics is simply wrong," and a conservative will answer right back, "Not at all, in fact, what *you* suggest we do is wrong." And it can go on like that forever. This is unfortunately the reality of policymaking and political debate. People are not usually willing to acknowledge that there is no one, objective morality. They assume that there is only one type of "right" and "wrong." They are not aware that there are two moral worldviews at the core of US politics, and that these two belief systems are equally "true" to those who endorse them, even if they conflict with each other and lead to contrasting policy proposals.

# Chapter 4

# Morality, Times Two
## How We Acquire and Navigate Two Moral Systems

### 4.1. The Physiology of Two Concepts:
### Social dominance and social empathy

**E.W.** It seems fair to say that the Strict Father and Nurturant Parent models are centered around the notions of social dominance and social empathy, respectively.

We've already discussed the fact that cognition is commonly rooted in the *physical* experiences we have during the first years of our lives.

It's easy to see how we acquire the notion of social dominance: Little Jack is physically stronger than Little Steve, and so Jack learns that he can use his physical strength to force his will onto his little playmate. The *physical* experience of dominating his playmate helps Jack learn the concept of *social* dominance.

In contrast, it seems that acquiring the concept of social empathy would be a less physical, somewhat more abstract endeavor that would require a more deliberate intervention: Little Jack is *told* by his father or mother that he ought to consider the feelings of other children.

One might wonder: do we have to be trained to be socially empathic, while the concept of social dominance is part of our human nature?

**G.L.** The answer is no, for the following reason. In 1991, a groundbreaking discovery was made in neuroscience. Vittorio Gallese and a team of neuroscientists at the University of Parma discovered what we call "mirror neurons."[25] These are neurons that fire in the brain whenever we carry out an action, or when we watch someone else carry out that same action. For instance, in our brains, the exact same neurons fire whether we're peeling a banana or we're watching someone else peel a banana. That's how these neurons got their name—they "mirror" actions.

**E.W.** Mirror neurons reside in the premotor cortex of our brains, which is the area that plans body movements, as well as in the area that regulates perceptual input, such as visual and audio information.

**G.L.** Right. Let's do a little exercise. Watch. Here, I'm picking up your pencil and holding it up. As you are watch me carry out this action, certain clusters of neurons are firing in your brain to help you *understand* the complex action I'm performing. So far so good. Now, go ahead and pick up that pencil yourself. As you do so, certain neurons in your brain are being activated to help you *carry out* this complex action. These are the same neurons that fired when you merely watched me pick up the pencil.

**E.W.** If those neurons are identical and activated in just the same way for both merely watching and actually performing an action, then humans should theoretically be constantly be mimicking every action they observe.

**G.L.** That's an important point. Yes, if the brain activity during watching and performing an action were *exactly* the same, we would copy each other's movements every single time we interacted. But that is not the case because while it is true that the same neurons fire, they are not activated with the same degree of intensity under both conditions. When

---

[25]   Rizzolatti et al. 1996; Gallese et al. 1996; Gallese 1999; Rizzolatti et al. 2000, 2001.

you are carrying out an action yourself, the neuron activation level is higher than when you're watching someone else carry out that action.

**E.W.** All right, but how do mirror neurons help Little Jack learn social empathy?

**G.L.** Well, two things are at play. First, there are connections in the brain between the region where mirror neurons reside and the region that manages emotions.

Second, we know that there is a "Physiology of Emotions" that is shared by people all over the world.[26] Every emotion goes hand in hand with specific facial muscle movements. When a person is happy, angry, or scared, their emotion comes hand in hand with an associated set of specific facial movements, such as "smiling" or "frowning."

How do people know that others are happy, sad, in pain, or angry, just by looking at them? Because of mirror neurons. Our brain notices even the tiniest muscle movements in our interlocutors' faces and, via mirror neurons, simulates what it means when we carry out those same movements.

**E.W.** So when we observe that a friend of ours is looking sad, our brain activates the same neurons it would be firing if *we* were looking sad.

This leaves us with an interesting conclusion. Namely, it's not our conscious decision whether or not to have empathy with others. We simply cannot help but empathize because our brains automatically copy the emotions that we witness in others.

**G.L.** Largely, yes. Mirror neurons are activated in our brains automatically. We have no control over this. Mirror neurons simulate what it would mean for ourselves if we acted out the facial muscle movements we see in our interlocutors. These neurons are connected to the emotional centers in our brains, which simulate the emotions that underlie the

---

[26] E.g., Ekman & Friesen 1969; Ekman 1985.

associated specific muscle movements. That's part of the equation.

In short, we understand other people's sadness, happiness, and fear via mimicking it. Some people speak of our intuitive understanding of others as "mind-reading." But in actuality, empathizing is enabled by a physical mechanism in our brain that is entirely automatic.

**E.W.** So let's say that Little Jack and Little Steve are at a playground going about their normal activities when they suddenly notice a crying Little Bob. While Jack keeps playing, Steve walks over to Bob, sits down with a concerned face, and tries to comfort him. If empathy is primarily an automatic physiological function, then why do some of us experience a higher degree of empathy than others?

**G.L.** One preliminary hypothesis goes something like this: the stronger the synaptic connection between mirror neurons and the emotional center in the brain, the more empathy a person experiences. This hypothesis makes sense because it explains how some people "learn" to be more empathic, namely, through being nurtured and treated with empathy by others. But there are other hypotheses as well. The details around neural simulation, mirror neurons, and empathy are still being studied.

**E.W.** Given that there are physical mechanisms that underlie empathy as well as dominance, let us revise the initial question: is social empathy more natural to humans than social dominance?

**G.L.** I really believe it would be a hopeless endeavor to try to hierarchize the two concepts in terms of their naturalness and degree of embodiment. Both are given by nature. Empathy is a natural function of our body, and is rooted in the physiology of our brain. And our understanding of the concept of social dominance is equally nature-given. It results from our early experiences that show us that some people are physically stronger than others and, as a result, can impose their will on them. Both concepts are rooted in physical experience. So the interesting question becomes, "Which concept dominates your life, and why?"

**E.W.** Well, the answer to that question should, at least in part, lie in our experiences with strict and nurturant family interactions. Let's talk about how the physical bases of social empathy and dominance show up in strict and nurturant family life.

Let's start with families that live by strict ideals. Fathers are grown men and are in general physically stronger than their wives and children, ergo, they are able to physically enforce their decisions.

**G.L.** Yes, they can make decisions about right and wrong, they can lay down rules of conduct, and they can physically enforce those rules if necessary. This is one of the ways in which Strict Father morality plays out in family life. And physical disputes—whether between a father and his children, or a father and mother—are not uncommon in families that live by strict ideals.

**E.W.** And a child who is repeatedly physically disciplined becomes increasingly familiar with the notion that physical dominance goes hand in hand with moral authority.

**G.L.** You bet. Now, in a Nurturant Parent family, the child learns empathic behavior by being treated with empathy. The moral authorities of the family unit model the behaviors they want to see in their children. Through their experiencing of nurturance and empathy, children begin to understand other people's emotional states and needs, and can respond to others in a nurturing way.

**E.W.** Simply put, a goal of Strict Father child-rearing is to make children strong and tough, while Nurturant Parent child-rearing strives to make children nurturers.

**G.L.** Yes. You see how these moral differences take us back to the question: "When your baby cries at night, do you pick him up?"

## 4.2. Morality, Times Two:
## Strict and Nurturant worldview

**E.W.** Strict Father and Nurturant Parent morality are highly complex models of reasoning, and they are based on our conceptualization of ideal families. Let's assume I grew up in a Strict Father family — will I ever be able to do a conceptual one-eighty and think about politics in terms of a Nurturant Parent worldview?

**G.L.** Absolutely. Say you grew up in a Strict Father family. You would still have been exposed to the Nurturant Parent model in other families, for instance at a friend's house.

**E.W.** Moreover, the two family models are omnipresent in our culture.

**G.L.** Right, we see them in real life, in movies, and last but not least, in political discourse. We are exposed to them on a daily basis, and thus we become familiar with both. This is why a 25-year-old environmental activist in Oregon can watch "Rocky I" through "Rocky VI", understand what these movies are about, and enjoy them. Although he probably lives his life mostly in terms of Nurturant Parent values, he still understands narrative structures that evolve around the Strict Father model.

**E.W.** If we understand both models equally well, then we can in theory make political decisions based on either of them. Which raises the question: who or what determines which model ultimately guides our policy stances?

**G.L.** The model we practice the most in our everyday lives, the one we regularly use as a template for our interactions with others, will usually be the one we apply to politics. The other model, which we may understand but don't regularly act on, will be less prominent in our minds, and therefore less likely to influence our decision-making with regard to political issues.

## 4.3. Torn By Principle: Biconceptualism

**E.W.** However, there are many people who use both models on a regular basis in their everyday lives. In the US, this is true for about a third of the population. For instance, there are Democrats who are largely morally progressive but in some areas of their lives they apply Strict Father morality.

**G.L.** Yes, those Democrats may apply Nurturant Parent ideals to politics and their family life, but resort to Strict Father ideals in their professional life, in the context of their career. Women in executive positions, for example, will often implement the Nurturant Parent model in their child-rearing practices but they might resort to a strict model in their professional lives.

And then there are Republicans who are largely morally conservative but in some areas of their lives they apply Nurturant Parent morality. They may be overall strict in politics, but love nature and thus endorse nurturant values when it comes to environmental policy. There are conservatives that live in progressive communities in which people take care of each other, nurture each other, and show high degrees of empathy for their neighbors. Finally, there are an increasing number of conservatives that are concerned with the health of their bodies and minds. They eat organic food, practice yoga, go to self-discovery seminars, and meditate during lunch breaks. These people may be strict in politics and professional life, but have a nurturant worldview when it comes to their own bodies and minds.

So yes, a large number of people endorse both models in different areas of their lives. They are able to reason in terms of both worldviews, and they actively apply them as they go about their lives.

**E.W.** And these "biconceptuals" may resort to either moral system when reasoning about politics. They are—at least somewhat—open to applying either worldview to politics.

And which value system they ultimately use depends largely on the language that governs public discourse.[27]

**G.L.** Exactly. And this is why you have to talk to biconceptuals in terms of your own value system. You need to be honest about the moral premises of your political goals and communicate issues accordingly. Progressives in the US, for instance, should use a nurturant moral worldview when discussing political issues. However, many progressives, at least in the US, do not always understand this mechanism or take it seriously enough. Conservatives, on the other hand, are more aware of the importance of moral communication. They are very good at communicating the moral premises of their programs. And not just since yesterday. They have been good at this for over three decades now — for 37 years, to be precise.

**E.W.** What happened 37 years ago?

**G.L.** It all started with the presidential elections in 1980. That year, Ronald Reagan ran against Jimmy Carter. These elections became a milestone in the history of conservative public discourse.

---

27   Lakoff 1996, 2004; Wehling 2013; Wehling et al. 2015.

# Chapter 5

# Deciding Politics
## Why People Vote Values

### 5.1. The Reagan Phenomenon:
### How to win against political interests

**E.W.** In 1980, Ronald Reagan beat Jimmy Carter in the presidential election, and he stayed in the Oval Office for eight years. What exactly was it about politics that Reagan understood but his Democratic opponents didn't get?

**G.L.** The whole thing happened like this: for his election campaign, Reagan had hired Richard Wirthlin as his chief strategist. Wirthlin had graduated from UC, Berkeley's economics department, and he was known to be an excellent pollster. And as an economics student at UC, Berkeley, he was taught a flawed assumption about how people make decisions. This assumption, which is still common among pollsters to this day, was that people vote for candidates based on the details of those candidates' positions on political issues.

So after being hired by Reagan, Wirthlin conducted a first poll on the popularity of his candidate. The result was bewildering: people hated Reagan's positions but they still wanted to vote for him. Wirthlin was shocked. He was Reagan's chief strategist, yet he had no clue why in heaven's name people wanted to vote for his candidate! So he got his team together and said: "Look guys, I honestly have no idea what's going on. But don't worry, I'll figure it out."

So he went ahead and analyzed how people reasoned about Reagan. And here's what he found out: people wanted to vote for Reagan because he talked about values, not just positions and programs. He openly discussed his moral viewpoints. People liked this, and they identified with his values. They felt that he was authentic and genuine, and that he could be trusted. People believed that he could be trusted as a leader who would act in accordance with his values. And so they wanted to vote for him despite the fact that they didn't share his political positions on single issues.

What did Reagan do after Wirthlin explained to him what he had found out? He ran his campaign on four things: values, trust, authenticity, and identity. And he discussed single political stances as exemplifying his values. Conservatives have stuck with this campaigning principle ever since.

**E.W.** Fine, so Reagan understood that people vote based on their values, not the specific details of issues. But what does this have to do with biconceptualism?

**G.L.** Well, take as an example the so-called Reagan Democrats. Those were blue-collar folks who were strict fathers at home but lived by nurturant values in their worker unions. So what did Reagan do to get their votes? He talked about politics in terms of family life and Strict Father values. And this is how he got biconceptuals, such as the Reagan Democrats, to cast their votes for him.

**E.W.** Give me an example of what it means to talk about political issues in terms of family life.

**G.L.** Sure. Take the national budget. A family-based argument would go along the lines of, "Look, you know that if your family budget runs low, you have to stop spending money. This is true also for the national budget, and this is why we need to cut social programs."

**E.W.** Cutting social programs could by no means have been reconcilable with the political interests of blue-collar workers.

**G.L.** Which is exactly the paradox we are talking about. So let's be precise: the father of a working class family in the Middle West has an objective interest in a strong social infrastructure, which could, for instance, allow his children to get a college degree. You present this guy with two party programs and ask, "Who represents your political interests better, the Democratic or the Republican candidate?" He might answer, "The Democratic one" — but he casts his vote for the Republican on Election Day. This is because we tend to vote primarily in terms of our moral worldview and values, and not in terms of our material self-interests.[28]

**E.W.** This is why someone who lives by the strict value system at home, raises his children in terms of its principles, and generally identifies with strict morality, will vote for a conservative candidate against his own economic interest.

**G.L.** And we see this all the time. Think about it. Tons of folks who are economically and socially disadvantaged vote conservative. Poor people, marginalized people, sick people, and people with little education vote conservative.

**E.W.** All the while a poor person would benefit from a robust welfare system. A marginalized person — whether based on ethnicity, sex, or gender — would benefit from policies that fight racism, sexism, homophobia, and so on. A sick person would benefit from a good public healthcare system. And, a person with a no educational background would benefit from a solid public school and higher education system.

**G.L.** Exactly. And yet, many of these folks vote conservative, which is against their own pronounced self-interest.

---

28    E.g., Miller 1999; Ratner & Miller 2001; Sears & Funk 1991; Shingles 1989.

## 5.2. Time to Backpedal:
## The political middle isn't there

**E.W.** What is the difference between biconceptuals and the political middle?

**G.L.** What political middle?

**E.W.** What do you mean?

**G.L.** I mean, what political middle? There's no such thing.

**E.W.** But political groups constantly fight for votes from the middle. One of the most agreed-upon campaign strategies is: move to the middle. This way, you will get both the votes from your primary base and those from people whose views are in between camps.

**G.L.** Well, progressives are the ones that fall into this trap. Conservatives don't "move toward the middle," and they have been winning elections just fine.

**E.W.** Let's be more precise — what's wrong with the political middle?

**G.L.** The political middle is a metaphor. It is a mental concept we use to reason about the electorate as lining up from the *far right* to the *far left*.

We say things like, "Where do you *stand* politically?" or, "As a young adult, I *moved* more and more *towards* the *left*." There is a notion that some issues are *left*-wing issues, while others are *right*-wing issues. Some people are *leftists*, and some *rightists*. People can be *left*-leaning on some issues and *right*-leaning on others. And so on.

**E.W.** Right. Agreeing with conservative policies places you more to the *right* on the political spectrum — metaphorically speaking, that is — and endorsing progressive policies situates you more to the *left*.

**G.L.** And this metaphoric mapping leads to the common misconception that if you are a politician on the left, and you want to get more votes than your base provides, then you need to move to the right.

Unfortunately, this is not a smart way to think about the electorate. And conservatives in the US understand this. They never move to the left to gain votes. They understand that people who are "in the middle" are *biconceptual* folks who to a part endorse a conservative worldview.

**E.W.** Conservatives know that many people who label themselves as independents, moderate progressives, or centrists agree to some extent with a conservative worldview and share conservative values. So the goal of conservatives becomes to activate the conservative worldview in voters' minds.

**G.L.** Precisely. And they do this by discussing political issues in terms of a strict moral worldview. They talk to the biconceptual "middle" in the same way in which they talk to their base. By doing so, they activate the conservative worldview in the minds of those voters, leading them to use that worldview as a basis for their political reasoning and participation.

**E.W.** And so conservatives stand their moral ground while progressive discourse in the US has moved markedly away from taking strong moral stances.

**G.L.** On the whole, yes. Although Barack Obama did an outstanding job with moral framing in 2008, Democrats in the US all in all don't promote their moral worldview enough. When discussing issues, they commonly adopt conservative language—and thereby conservative ideas! By doing this, they evoke and strengthen the conservative worldview in people's minds. They propagate conservative values by integrating them into their own discourse.

**E.W.** The result is that they unwittingly help conservatives gain political power and win elections.

**G.L.** Yes, because regardless of what progressives might believe, people vote values, not self-interests.

### 5.3. The End of Rationalism:
### Why there are no rational voters

**E.W.** So in essence, we just denied people the ability to rationally pursue their self-interests.

**G.L.** Indeed. But really, to have a conversation about "rationally" pursuing things in life, we need to first discuss rationalism. Rationalism poses a huge problem in politics.

**E.W.** How can rationalism be a problem in politics? It's the very principle on which democratic organization rests.

**G.L.** Rationalism is a problem because many people still believe that its espoused principles are true.

Many folks who are active in politics in this country got their degrees in fields such as Political Science and Law. And one thing you learn early on when you study these subjects is that the ideals of this nation — its political and legal system — are based on the Enlightenment.

**E.W.** The central concept of the Enlightenment was rationalism, namely the idea that all humans are rational beings and that it is our rationality that distinguishes us from other species.

**G.L.** Yes, the idea was that rationality and reason are inherent to the human race, and therefore all people can reason in a rational way and make their own rational decisions. This is why we should govern ourselves, and why we no longer have to ask kings or popes what to do.

**E.W.** Okay. But now we're questioning the notion that people are rational beings?

**G.L.** We better. The theory of rationalism implies a number of assumptions about human thought that are incorrect. We discussed them earlier in our conversation. Here are the fallacies: thought is conscious; thought is literal and mirrors the world per se, as it objectively exists; and, thought is universal and we all reason in the same way.

Well, cognitive science research has shown that these assumptions are outdated. It has shown that thought is largely unconscious,[29] that it depends on mental structures such as metaphors,[30] and that people reason differently based on the cognitive templates their minds acquired through their cultural and individual experiences.[31] Modern-day research on human reasoning and decision-making contradicts the core notions of traditional rationalism. So, yes: rationalism is a myth.

### 5.4. Facts Need Frames:
### The nonsense of purely factual communication

**E.W.** Assuming that people automatically reason according to rationalist theory can seriously interfere with political communication and participation. Just consider what rationalism implies for polling. Political rationalism assumes that people are conscious of their reasoning, that they will rationally decide what lies in their best interest, and that they will be able to tell you what their political decisions are based on.

**G.L.** Exactly. It assumes that people should be able to tell you their rational stances on, say, taxation. Moreover, you should be able to ask someone in a pre-election poll, "What are the most pressing issues for you?" and that person should be able to tell you. And then you can make sure to include all those issues in your program and campaigning.

The rational voter will then vote for you, because you are addressing the issues that are in his or her best interests.

---

29   E.g., Higgins 1996; Kahneman & Tversky 1984; Rock 2005; Thibodeau & Boroditsky 2011.
30   E.g., Gibbs 1994, 2006; Lakoff & Johnson 1980, 1999; Moeller et al. 2008; Zhong & Liljenquist 2006.
31   E.g., Boroditsky 2001; Boroditsky et al. 2003; Casasanto & Jasmin 2010; Casasanto 2014; Nuñez & Sweetser 2006; Oppenheimer & Trail 2010.

In this scenario, there is only one possible reason for people to *not* support the party that represents their interests: a lack of information, and a lack of factual knowledge about issues and how to tackle them. And so the best way to communicate with the electorate is to provide them with facts — many, many facts.

**E.W.** So political communication that draws on rationalistic principles is "delusional" in that it assumes people will base their political decisions on facts.

**G.L.** Yes. And progressives in the US commonly operate in this way. While conservatives talk a great deal about morality and values, progressives tend to talk about facts and program details.

**E.W.** In listening to you, one might start to wonder whether facts are obsolete in political participation.

**G.L.** No, they are not. But the processing of facts relies on larger cognitive structures that give facts their meaning. Facts do not have meaning "per se". Facts become meaningful as our minds integrate them into larger interpretative templates. Such templates are called "frames".[32] Facts cannot be processed outside of frames. So if you want to communicate the pressing relevance of certain political facts, then the first thing you want to do is make sure that you're using frames in which those facts actually make sense.

**E.W.** Moreover, you want to make sure that you don't evoke in people's minds the frames being used by your opponent, because most likely those frames are not consistent with the facts *you* regard as important.

**G.L.** And so you must choose your frames carefully, because once a frame is activated in someone's mind, facts that don't fit into this frame will be ignored at first.[33]

---

[32] E.g., Fillmore 1976, 1985; Goffman 1974; Minsky 1974.
[33] E.g., Stanfield & Zwaan 2001; Yaxley & Zwaan 2007.

So yes, facts are important. How could they not be important, especially in politics?

**E.W.** But if the facts don't fit the cognitive frame, they won't generate a whole lot cognitive pull.

**G.L.** Even worse, they might "bounce off" the frame and not be considered by the listener at all.

Chapter 6

# Political Framing
## Value Laden Words

### 6.1. The Brain's Filter: Frames and facts

**E.W.** In January 2006, the *New York Times* ran an interesting headline: "Shocker! Partisan Reasoning is Unconscious!"[34] The article reported results from a study that tested voters' awareness of lies in politics. Thirty adults—half of them Republicans, the other half Democrats—listened to statements by George W. Bush and John Kerry. In those statements, both politicians contradicted themselves—they lied. While subjects immediately detected that the other camp's candidate was making inconsistent statements, they were unaware of the fact that their own candidate wasn't telling the truth either!

**G.L.** Well, what the *New York Times* labeled a "shocker" in 2006 is somewhat old news. For about four decades now, we have known that people reason in terms of frames. Every time we think—any thought at all—our brain activates a frame. Frames are cognitive configurations that structure our world knowledge and make sense of information.

There are frames that we use in language. And then there are deep-seated cognitive frames that structure our thoughts. One can think of those frames as establishing what's

---

[34] "A Shocker: Partisan Thought is Unconscious," *New York Times*, 1/24/2006.

"common sense" to us—what we believe to be true about the world.

Now, facts that are not in line with our "common sense" understanding of the world will, figuratively speaking, bounce off our deep-seated frames. They don't enter into our reasoning because they have no place in the frames that govern our perceptions of the world, or, in this case, our perception of a political leader or candidate.

**E.W.** So given these facts about human cognition, it's not at all surprising to see that the participants in the reported study didn't get the fact that "their" leader was lying. That fact simply had no place in the frames that structured their general perceptions of the person in question.

If you think about it, the influence that frames exert on our perception of the world is quite startling. Can't we avoid using frames altogether and return to a "pure," more rational way of perceiving the world?

**G.L.** That's impossible. We can't understand things in the world outside of cognitive frames, nor can we comprehend language without frames.

In order to process language, we automatically activate frames. We neurally[35] and mentally[36] simulate the concepts that we read or hear—actions, images, and so on. If I say to someone, "John lifted the glass and drank the water," then my interlocutor comprehends this sentence by activating a frame. This frame includes a number of inferences about what it means to "drink a glass of water." For instance, it mentally invokes a simulation of the motor-movement that is necessary to lift up a glass of water and to drink from that glass. If my interlocutor were unable to imagine these things, then the sentence would have no meaning for him or her.

So, in order to reason in any meaningful way, we need frames that tell us what given actions, and so on, "mean" in the context of our world knowledge.

---

[35]  E.g., Desai et al. 2010; Pulvermueller 2001, 2002; Tettamanti et al. 2005.
[36]  E.g., Matlock 2004; Zwaan et al. 2002; Zwaan & Pecher 2012.

**E.W.** Cognitive science holds that frames, like metaphors, are grounded in the structures of our brains and strengthened via repetition. If you hear a frame over and over again, then your brain develops the neural circuitry that manifests and reinforces that frame in your mind. The more often it gets activated, the more it is strengthened over time.

**G.L.** And the stronger a frame gets, the more it becomes part of your common sense. And facts that don't fit within our commonsensical frames will usually be ignored.

**E.W.** That means facts themselves will rarely change how we reason about the world. Conceptual change occurs through the activation and strengthening of alternative frames.

**G.L.** Right. "Changing one's mind" means to activate alternative frames, for instance such frames that lend new meaning and urgency to political facts and information that would otherwise remain ignored.

And one can reason in terms of contradictory frames that interpret facts in entirely different ways. We have frames in our brains that contradict each other completely, yet we can reason in terms of these divergent frames just fine. However, we can never activate contradictory frames simultaneously.

### 6.2. The Dog that was a Man:
### Frames and perception

**E.W.** Why not evaluate ideas through all applicable frames *simultaneously* to formulate the most informed understanding and conclusions?

**G.L.** Because it's impossible to simultaneously activate contradictory frames. When one frame is activated in your mind, the activation of opposing frames is being blocked. This is called mutual inhibition.

Let's look at a classic example of how our minds process information through divergent frames. Look, I'm getting a pencil and paper, and drawing a three-dimensional cube. First, I'm drawing a square. Then I draw another square that is the same size but is positioned partially behind the first one. Now I'm drawing four lines that connect the corresponding corners of the two squares. See, just like this. Now we have a transparent, three-dimensional cube. As you look at it, you can perceive it in two ways: you can see either of the two squares as being the cube's *front*. And depending on which square you see as being in the *front*, you are looking at a cube that is either tilting up or down.

The fascinating thing is that we can see two different versions of the box or cube, and we can jump back and forth between them. However, we can never see both views at the same time. Our brain needs a moment to "shut down" the first interpretation before it can redirect its energy flow towards activating the other interpretation.

This is a good example of how the frames in our minds determine what we see and how we experience the world.

**E.W.** And if we both look at the cube again right now, you might be looking at an upright cube while I'm seeing a cube that's lying down.

**G.L.** If that were the case, we would be employing different frames to process the same visual information.

**E.W.** This is reminiscent of the "impossible constructions" by Dutch artist Maurits Cornelius Escher. Escher drew buildings that at first sight seemed to be no more than regular architectural structures, but at second sight turned out to be structurally impossible — because some aspects of their assemblies were contradictory. The constructions depicted in Escher's drawings can never be fully comprehended.

**G.L.** Exactly, the observer has to constantly switch frames. There are many of these types of "optical illusions," which, in reality, are simply products of the mutual inhibition mechanism in our brain. You might have seen the drawing that depicts both a man's head and a dog. Both things are present in the drawing — a man and a dog. But because the two interpretations of the visual input contradict each other, our brain picks one over the other at any given moment in time. We can switch between the two interpretations. We might first see a dog, and then see the man, and then the dog again. But we can never see both things simultaneously. It's cognitively impossible. Our brain can only activate one of two contradictory frames at a time.

Let's go back to an issue you raised a moment ago — namely, the question of whether we can think without using frames. Imagine someone who has never seen nor heard of a dog. That person would have no visual frame for the concept "dog" and would, therefore, not be able to perceive the dog in the drawing. For such a person, the drawing would depict only a man because the person wouldn't have a frame for conceiving of a dog.

**E.W.** So we all hold different and often contradictory frames in our minds. The way we process facts depends on what frame is active in our mind at a given moment. If a fact fits with a frame that is already active in our minds or is part of what we perceive as common sense, then it's easily understood. If a fact doesn't fit into whatever frame is already activated and is not a part of our common sense, then it will not be readily understood.

**G.L.** Yes, and if you have developed alternate frames, you can switch from one frame to another, and facts that seemed irrelevant through the first frame can become highly meaningful in the alternate one.

### 6.3. Don't Try *Not* to Think:
### Frames and negation

**E.W.** Let's talk about frame negation. And what better way to get into this topic than ask: what's the story behind your book title, *Don't Think of an Elephant?*[37]

**G.L.** That title refers to a classic example from psychology that I use when teaching introductory courses to cognitive linguistics. I've been using this example for over twenty

---

[37]   Lakoff 2004.

years now, and it doesn't get old. So here's what I do. I tell my students, "Be quiet folks. There's something I need you to do for me, so listen up." I wait until the class is quiet, and then I say, "All right then, here we go. I need you to go ahead and do the following for me: don't think of an elephant!"...

...Of course, they can't do it.

**E.W.** Because in order to comprehend what *not* to think about, you need to first activate the image of whatever it is that you're not supposed to think about—otherwise, you won't know what not to think about! So you mentally simulate the negated idea,[38] and not only that, you also neurally simulate it[39]—the circuits that constitute the idea in your brain show activation!

**G.L.** And so when I tell students, "Don't think of an elephant," they automatically activate a frame that encompasses whatever it is they know about elephants. Negating an idea means activating that idea. Always.

**E.W.** And not only that, the negated concept also gets strengthened in the listener's mind, because activating a frame strengthens it. This is the "Hebbian learning" mechanism we talked about earlier.

**G.L.** Indeed. So if it actually were my intention to not have my students think of elephants, then telling them to *not* think of elephants would essentially be just as bad as telling them "Listen up! I want everyone to think of elephants." Either way, they would think of elephants, and the frame circuitry that represents their knowledge about elephants would be strengthened.

**E.W.** In other words, if you started each class of the semester by saying "Don't think of an elephant," then your students would involuntarily build cognitive muscle for that frame in their minds.

---

38  Kaup et al. 2006, 2007.
39  Foroni & Semin 2013; Tettamanti et al. 2008; Tomasino et al. 2010.

**G.L.** Yes. Now, I happen to really not care about whether or not my students constantly think of elephants, and neither do they probably. But when it comes to politics, well, that's a whole different thing. In politics, the question of what frames are evoked and strengthened in people's minds is a crucial matter.

**E.W.** Hold on. Before we get into politics, let's revisit the most important framing facts we discussed thus far: every word evokes a frame. Every negation of a frame activates that frame. Activating a frame means to cognitively and neurally strengthen it. Frames that are strengthened via constant linguistic repetition become common sense, which means that we no longer question the validity of those frames and accept them as, well, objectively right and real. All of this is largely unconscious. Moreover, we cannot simultaneously think about issues in terms of frames that contradict each other. And we ignore facts that don't fit into the frames we are using at a given point in time.

**G.L.** And it's important to recognize the relevance of these findings for politics and public discourse. It really can't be overestimated!

In the US, for instance, conservatives do a great job of implementing their own frames in public debate, while progressives lag behind in terms of proactively framing issues in terms of their worldview. Moreover, progressives often negate the frames that conservatives use. They constantly get caught up in arguing *against* conservative ideas. And they lack a well-functioning communication infrastructure that ensures adequate, moral framing of issues across progressive groups on a daily basis. Conservatives are just much better organized when it comes to these things.

**E.W.** No doubt, conservatives have understood the importance of moral communication, and they have done a great job with it. They have a very healthy communication infrastructure that ensures that their frames get out there into public discourse. Take FOX News, for example. Many people in the US watch this channel and take it very seriously. And what is being said on FOX News often sets the general tone for the frames that are then used in more moderate public debates. Conservatives tend to frame issues in terms of their values.

**G.L.** Yes, conservatives get people to reason about issues in terms of conservative morality, and they strengthen that worldview in the public mind. Progressives don't do this in the same way. They are not as concerned with understanding the moral foundations of their positions on issues and then communicating those foundations clearly. They often work by the credo "The facts will set you free." Sadly, that credo does not pan out.

**E.W.** Because facts are important, but they have no inherent morality. Facts in and of themselves do not tell us what is right or wrong, or whether something is good or bad. Frames do this job.

**G.L.** And the moral frames that political parties resort to when *reasoning* about issues lend meaning to facts. And those frames, in turn, have to be used when *communicating* issues.

Conservatives have a whole battery of frames that construe issues in terms of conservative morality. And as long as progressives use those frames, their own moral concerns will not get through to people, and facts they believe to be crucial for policymaking will remain ignored by the public mind. Progressives need to be much more focused on developing their own moral frames for issues, and they really need to stop it with the fact lists.

### 6.4. The Laden Tax Debate:
### Conservative taxation frames

**E.W.** Let's get specific and look at an example of such moral framing in political debate. Take a classic example, the phrase "tax relief." This is a frame that fits with Strict Father ideals.

**G.L.** Why? Because, in this frame, taxes are metaphorically a burden that you can be relieved from; therefore taxes are bad. And in the eyes of conservatives, taxes are in fact a burden to people, and taxation is something that limits people's freedom. Speaking of "tax relief" is in sync with that perspective.

Within this frame, tax increases are by definition bad, because they further burden and harm citizens. Tax cuts, in contrast, are by definition good, because they relieve us.

**E.W.** Conservatives are being truthful when using this frame — taxation is seen as de facto bad according to Strict Father morality, because taxes get in the way of economic and social competition.

**G.L.** Right. In the Strict Father worldview, high taxes are an immoral punishment of self-discipline. What the "tax relief" frame hides, though, is the fact that people who are economically successful have built that success largely on the basis of the tax-supported public infrastructure.

**E.W.** What would be an alternative frame, on that fits with Nurturant Parent morality?

**G.L.** Well, progressives in the US should talk about taxation in terms of the commonwealth principle. They should talk about the fact that individual success, liberty, and happiness rely on the public infrastructure that we all built and are maintaining together.

They should talk about the fact that those who use this infrastructure the most—to run their businesses and make a profit—should give back more than others.

They could also talk about the fact that contributing taxes partly means to simply give back what the government has already invested in you. Once that frame is established, the question is: are you paying back your dues, or are you trying to get a free ride?

Linguistic frames that would stem from this type of moral reasoning would define the issue of taxation in entirely different terms!

## 6.5. What is it We're Debating?
### Issue defining frames

**E.W.** By using certain frames in public discourse, we define what a given issue *is about*. We define what it is that we are debating — long before we get into the details of the debates, long before the battle over solutions, facts, and details ever start!

**G.L.** Absolutely. There are frames that decide what our political issues are. These are issue-defining frames. They establish what it is we are debating.

**E.W.** And issue-defining frames are incredibly powerful. They set the stage by defining ahead of time which facts and pieces of information will be considered to be part of the "plot" of an issue discussion, and which ones will not even be mentioned in the script.

**G.L.** Let's take immigration as an example. Immigration is an important issue in the US, and the issue can be framed in two ways. For one, you can call it "illegal immigration," and then the issue becomes whether or not an immigrant entered the US legally. Or, you can call it "illegal employment," and then the issue lies with the employers in the US that offer illegal immigrants illegal work to make a hefty profit off of them.

Or, take the domestic surveillance legislations in the US after 9/11. When the Bush Administration first introduced the legislation, they named it "Terrorist Surveillance Program." If that frame had stuck, then anyone who criticized the legislation would have been "against terrorist surveillance." That would have made it very hard to express any opposition to the program.

Well, the label that ultimately prevailed was "Domestic Surveillance Program." That was a very different frame, and it defined the issue that was being debated as an issue of protecting the freedom and privacy of US citizens.

**E.W.** Progressives in the US have not been this lucky when it comes to the abortion debate. Anti-abortion advocates are commonly referred to as "pro-life" advocates.

**G.L.** This frame comes from conservative anti-abortion advocates. And from their moral perspective, this is a great frame. Just consider for a moment the rich inferential structure it provides for our reasoning. Think about the ways in which it defines those folks who are against banning abortions. They are either "anti-life" or "pro-death"!

**E.W.** The "pro-life" frame defines the issue we are debating: it's an issue of life and death for the so-called "unborn child."

**G.L.** However, this is only one of many possible ways to frame the debate. Another very legitimate way to frame the debate would be to talk about the freedom of women to make their own life decisions, and ask: should men or the government be allowed to make decisions about women's bodies and thereby violate their basic human right to liberty from oppression and protection from harm? A framing that highlights the latter as the moral dilemma at hand would be a much better and more accurate way of communicating what this issue is about from a *progressive* viewpoint. And that frame, in turn, would lend meaning and urgency to the facts that progressives believe are relevant.

### 6.6. Values to be Mindful of:
### Conservative and progressive worldviews

**E.W.** Public common sense in the US has tilted quite a bit towards the right over the past decades. Given what we discussed just now, there seems to be only one way for progressives to re-establish a conceptual alternative—through progressive moral framing of the issues we face, whether those are abortion, the environment, the economy, welfare, or taxation, to name only a few.

**G.L.** Yes. Every political argument ought to start with a moral premise, with an answer to the question: what is morally right or wrong policymaking on this issue?

Issue stances are symbolic of the moral stances we hold. They are an outcome of one's moral worldview and therefore must be communicated as such. However, a lot of folks believe that positions are "values" in and of themselves. They mistake their positions for their values.

**E.W.** That's true. When asked what their values are, politically involved people will often answer, "My values are environmental protection, public healthcare, and social equality."

**G.L.** Well, those are not values. Those are merely positions that share a common moral basis, they *stem* from one and the same moral worldview, which in this case is probably a progressive Nurturant Parent worldview with the central values of empathy, nurturance, and individual as well as social responsibility.

If you seek political support, then you need to speak about your values as clearly as you can, because your values are what distinguishes you from your political opponent.

**E.W.** Simply put, it does not suffice to just tell people what you will do. You need to tell them *why* you are going to do it, that is, why the actions you propose are a moral necessity.

**G.L.** And once progressives have become accustomed to discussing issues in terms of their moral worldview on an everyday basis, they will have a much easier time finding good slogans for day-to-day issues and campaigns.

Right now, conservative slogans still tend to be cognitively more powerful. They tend to be really good because conservatives have done the communicative groundwork for decades now.

**E.W.** They have established public moral narratives that tell a very convincing story, and in that story conservatives are the good guys and progressives are the bad guys.

**G.L.** Oh yes, conservatives have established great over-arching moral frames in public discourse. Those frames have turned into deep-seated cognitive templates in people's minds. Now all that's left for conservatives to do is to find slogans that tap into those larger moral templates.

There's only one way to reclaim a progressive common sense as an alternative to the conservative common sense that currently sets the tone in many of our debates. Progressives must start speaking about their values more — across issues and over long periods of time.

**E.W.** Yet one couldn't hope to turn an ultraconservative into a progressive by discussing the political menu of the day in terms of nurturant values.

**G.L.** Bear in mind that we all *understand* the strict and nurturant worldview. Some of us use one and the same worldview in all areas of our lives, including politics. But others don't. Up to a third of the electorate in the US is biconceptual.[40] These folks endorse both family models, and they can resort to either when making political decisions.

Biconceptuals will be open to seeing matters from either moral worldview, so when political leaders are communicating with that part of the electorate, it's extremely important to speak about one's values.

**E.W.** Even though biconceptuals will not be able to apply two conflicting moral frames at once, they are somewhat open to using either one.

**G.L.** Yes. They will give priority to the worldview that public debate evokes more strongly in their minds.[41]

### 6.7. The Manipulated Brain:
### Framing versus propaganda

**E.W.** Let's be honest. Framing is a way to manipulate people, to mess with their reasoning and decision-making. A

---

[40]   Lakoff 1996, 2004; Wehling 2013; Wehling et al. 2015.
[41]   Ibid.

modern form of propaganda, by dint of cognition and neuroscience research.

**G.L.** No, it's not. We all reason and speak in terms of frames. Whenever we communicate, we use frames, no matter what the goal of our communication is. So if you are in politics and your goal is to be an honest and effective communicator of your political ideals and programs, then you better invest in finding the right frames!

**E.W.** But propaganda clearly uses targeted framing as well.

**G.L.** Of course! But propaganda is undemocratic and seeks to manipulate. And if we consider the things we have discussed thus far, we see why propaganda is so effective—it changes people's brains.

Propaganda is per definition undemocratic, but that's not true for regular public discourse in Western societies, where there are multiple moral worldviews at play and good framing is needed wherever people seek to be honest about their morality and make it accessible as a template for political action.

**E.W.** Still, the boundary between propaganda and framing seems to lie in somewhat muddy waters.

**G.L.** Not necessarily. When conservatives talk about lowering the "tax burden," all they are doing is being honest in describing their point of view. That's not propaganda or manipulation. One might not like the way they reason about taxes, but that doesn't mean they're being undemocratic.

**E.W.** The problem is not that some political groups speak their moral mind, but that others fail to speak *their* moral mind.

**G.L.** Absolutely.

Chapter 7

# "God Bless America"
## Religion, Metaphor, and Politics

### 7.1. "Our Father...":
### Metaphors for God

**E.W.** There are religious groups in the US and elsewhere who claim that their actions—including their religiously motivated political actions—are aligned exactly with the wording of a holy script. This pretense implies that religious scripts, such as the Bible, have literal meaning per se.

**G.L.** They don't. One thing is crystal clear: we reason about God in terms of metaphor.[42] The concept of God—any God—is abstract. Whenever we read holy scripts, we interpret them. When we read a passage from the Bible, we have to interpret it in one way or another. Our minds can only make sense of God in metaphoric terms.

People who claim to be following the literal word of the Bible are mistaken. No doubt, there are people who wholeheartedly *believe* that they are following the literal word of a holy script. But it's simply not possible.

**E.W.** Are you denying God's existence?

**G.L.** Why would I deny God's existence?

**E.W.** Because you are saying that God only exists in metaphor.

---

[42] E.g., Lakoff 1996; Meier et al. 2007; Stec & Sweetser 2013.

**G.L.** Let's talk about metaphor and truth. Earlier, we talked about the fact that certain abstract ideas, such as nationhood, are naturally reasoned and talked about in terms of domains with which we have direct world experience, such as family. We can't touch, smell, taste, or see nations per se, so we reason about nations in terms of metaphor. But does that mean that the notion of nationhood is arbitrary and unreal? Is there, in actuality, no such thing as a nation? Of course there is! But our brains happen to function in such a way that we reason about things we can't physically perceive largely in terms of metaphoric mappings—automatically and unconsciously.

The fact that we understand many things in the world via metaphor doesn't mean that these things are less real.

**E.W.** And this goes for God, too. God is an entity that lies outside of our direct perception. Our conceptual system perceives of Him largely through metaphoric mappings.

**G.L.** Some years ago, a student from the Graduate Theological Union came to my course on metaphorical thought and asked to take it. I said, "Of course, but why?" He replied, "God is ineffable. We can only understand God through metaphor. I want to know how we do it."

This doesn't make God any less real or more real. Just like the fact that we reason about nations in terms of metaphor doesn't make nations less real! But if we take the metaphors literally, they can affect our behavior.

**E.W.** There are many metaphors for God. There's the notion that *God is a shepherd* and *we're His flock of sheep*. There's *God as a King* and *we as His subjects*. There's *God as teacher* and *we as students*.

**G.L.** Another common mapping is *God as a war commander* and *His followers as warriors*. This metaphor has led to a lot of suffering in the history of mankind.

But the most central metaphor we engage in when reasoning about God is *God as a father* and *believers as His children*.

**E.W.** As the Gospel of Matthew declares, "Your *father* knows what you need before you ask him. This is how you are to pray: Our *Father* in heaven…"

**G.L.** Voila! This is a classic example of the *God As Father* metaphor. It's used across religions. Christianity, Islam, and Judaism all share this mapping as a central conceptualization of divinity. And if we speak about God as a father, then we reason about Him as a father. And our religiously motivated actions in everyday life as well as in politics will be in line with this reasoning.

So if we reason about God as a parental figure, then the interesting question becomes: what type of parent is He?

### 7.2. Moral Religion: How God's commandments arise from our embodied mind

**E.W.** Many people see religion as the source of moral values. For many, religion defines what is moral and immoral action.

**G.L.** It's true that many people see religion as a source of morality. That's a very common assumption, but it's not entirely correct. Morality and religion are closely connected, but in a different way. Our sense of morality does not directly emanate from religion. It originates outside of religion, as part of our general cognitive development.

We acquire a system of metaphors for morality through our experiences in the world — in our families and in society. It's not religion in itself that tells us what constitutes moral and immoral behavior. It's the other way around: we unconsciously map our reasoning about morality *onto* religion and religious scripts. That's an important fact. Since the beginning of time, religions have been formed and changed by people's moral beliefs and reasoning, which largely originate outside of religion.

**E.W.** So religious values come about as we interpret a given religion in terms of our moral beliefs.

**G.L.** And because we hold different beliefs about right and wrong, we can hold different sets of religious values. Those values then will guide our religious reasoning and actions. But how exactly do we map our moral beliefs onto religion?

**E.W.** First of all, in any given religion, we must select a metaphor for God.

**G.L.** The most common one is *God As Father*. So let's assume you use that metaphor. You conceptualize God as a parental figure. Now you have to decide what kind of parent He is going to be, what behaviors He wants to foster in you, and how He will teach you to be a good kid.

**E.W.** In short, we—unconsciously—have to decide whether our Heavenly Father is a strict or nurturant parent, and what will count as "good" and "bad" behavior in His eyes.

**G.L.** Exactly. And see, when you go to Hebrew school and you are being taught the Torah, you're not just being taught the literal text itself. The meaning of the Torah only exists in the context of its interpretations. And those interpretations can be contradictory.

### 7.3. Abraham and Isaac:
### ...and the moral of the story?

**E.W.** You say this is true for all religious scripts. How about an example from the Bible?

**G.L.** Let's take as an example a story from the Old Testament that's relevant not just for Christians—it's the story of Abraham and Isaac. I was taught this story as a young boy in school.

**E.W.** And that story goes roughly like this: God asks Abraham to sacrifice his son Isaac. As Abraham is about to kill his son, God sends an angel telling him to sacrifice a sheep instead.

**G.L.** Correct. That's the central plot of the narrative. But we have to engage in interpretation of this narrative in order to give it meaning. We have to make sense of the story beyond the described actions.

**E.W.** True. So what story was it that you were taught as a young boy in school?

**G.L.** The interpretation that I learned in school is this: God told Abraham to sacrifice his son Isaac, but He didn't expect Abraham to actually kill his own son. He was just testing him. He wanted to see whether Abraham knew how to be a good Jew. And as a good Jew, Abraham should have replied, "No way! I'm not killing my son! My faith tells me not to do so."

But Abraham got it wrong. He was really going to kill his own son. So God in heaven said, "Hold on, you're not really...! Good gracious! What are you doing? A good father doesn't kill his own son!" And in order to keep Abraham from doing so, God had to quickly send an angel who said to Abraham, "Stop it, you fool! That's not what a good Jew is supposed to do! You got it wrong! Kill the sheep!"

**E.W.** The story I was taught in my German elementary school was a different one. I was taught that God really *meant* what He said: God ordered Abraham to sacrifice his son because He wanted to see whether Abraham would obey Him. This was to test Abraham's faith in God. If Abraham were a good Jew, he would obey God's word, no matter what. He would believe that God knew best what would be the right thing to do.

**G.L.** And since Abraham loved God very much, his desire to abide by God's word was stronger than his love for Isaac. Thus, he was willing to sacrifice his son for God. When he was about to do so, God had proof that Abraham would abide by His authority completely, even at the cost of killing his son. In other words, God saw that Abraham was a good Jew. So to reward Abraham for his loyalty and obedience, He quickly sent an angel who said, "Good news, Abraham!

You have proven to God that you are a good Jew who is willing to abide by His word without question. And, as a reward, you may keep you son Isaac... Kill the sheep instead."

By the way, something that both stories have in common is that, in the end, the sheep gets the short end of the stick!

**E.W.** The two stories offer two different answers to the question of what makes Abraham a good Jew. In the first interpretation, which is the nurturant version, God is testing Abraham's moral compass—his ability to make morally right decisions.

**G.L.** Yes, and the only right way for Abraham to react to God's bizarre request is to refuse to kill his own child. Under any circumstances, his decision should be to *not* kill his son, even at the prospect of upsetting God. He is *not* supposed to blindly follow God's word. He's supposed to catch on to the fact that God's command is off.

**E.W.** In the second version, which is the strict version, God expects absolute obedience from Abraham.

**G.L.** Right, God expects him not to question His word. "Father knows best!" There's only one right way for Abraham to react to God's query, and that is to be willing to kill Isaac if God wants him to. And because he is about to do exactly as he was told, he is being rewarded.

**E.W.** So the bottom line is: the story of Abraham and Isaac has no moral! Not one moral per se, anyway. The moral of the story depends on which worldview you employ to interpret the plot. Similarly, then, the Bible must have different morals for conservative and progressive Christians in the US.

**G.L.** Indeed. Conservative Christians tend to conceptualize God as a strict father, and progressives view Him as a nurturant parent.

### 7.4. Religious Politics:
### For whose God's sake?

**E.W.** The US Pledge of Allegiance says, "...one nation under God, indivisible, with Liberty and Justice for all." Well, we just established that America is actually a nation under *two* Gods. Let's talk about the God that a conservative president is calling upon when he says, "God bless America."

**G.L.** The Strict Father God has a very rigid system of reward and punishment. If you are obedient to Him, you will go to heaven. If you aren't, then you'll go to hell. The threat of punishment makes you follow God's rules.

The core theme is God's absolute authority. People who follow God's strict rules are good Christians—they have overcome their inner evil and learned self-discipline.

**E.W.** And God cannot simply give people salvation on a silver platter. If He did, we would have no incentive to become morally strong and disciplined.

**G.L.** Right. We would simply give in to immorality, because we are weak by nature. Therefore, we have to earn salvation.

**E.W.** What if we see God as a Nurturant Parent figure?

**G.L.** The nurturant God offers us grace, and God's grace is metaphorically construed as nurturance. God looks out for us and cares for us. We cannot earn His grace, nurturance and care. He gives those things unconditionally.

It pleases God when we care for others. We must help others, just as God helps us. We must nurture others, just as God nurtures us.

By the way, Jesus takes on an important role in this progressive interpretation of Christianity. He is the one who showed us what God expects from us, and the more we live our lives by the example of Jesus, the closer to God we can be.

**E.W.** What's more, Jesus taught us to be tolerant when He said, "Judge not, that you be not judged!"

**G.L.** And we ought to be fair—"Let him who is without sin cast the first stone." We ought to not be violent—"Turn the other cheek." We ought not to seek to dominate others—"Blessed are the meek: for they shall inherit the earth."

**E.W.** And we should help others, especially those who are in dire need of our help, such as the sick, the needy, and the poor.

However, if we don't live by the example of Jesus, then God shows His strict face and sends us to hell for all eternity.

**G.L.** Well, the notions of heaven and hell are less central in the nurturant interpretation of Christianity. Instead, there's more focus on the concepts of forgiveness and restitution.

If we stray from God's moral path by not looking out for others or harming them, then we are guilty of sin and God is disappointed. But the nurturant version of God is merciful, and He grants us forgiveness. And we should in turn offer our forgiveness to others: "...forgive us our trespasses, as we forgive those who trespass against us."

**E.W.** I wonder, can't religiously motivated politics be independent of moral templates like strict and nurturant morality? Is there really no unbiased, independent, morality-free way of applying religion to politics?

**G.L.** Are you asking for religious politics that are morally unbiased? Well, that's not possible, because there is no such thing as neutral religion. Religion *depends* on moral interpretation. The Bible in and of itself gives us no hint as to what would constitute moral politics in the name of God. It's only through the interpretation of Holy Scripture—through a strict or nurturant lens—that you get a guideline for moral politics in the name of religion.

### 7.5. God's Favorite Children:
### The necessary objectivism of holy scripts

**E.W.** A lot of people still assume that religions have one objective morality written down in holy scripts. For anyone who holds that assumption, people who follow those scripts most closely are the religion's "topnotch" believers, God's favorites.

Put differently, if you assume that morality emerges from religion, then the question of whether you are *moral* becomes a question of whether you are *religious*. When you assume that morality emerges from religion, and every religious script therefore carries only one, objectively right morality, then those who most closely abide by the script can claim moral high grounds.

**G.L.** In which case the more Bible-abiding your politics, the more morally "right" you objectively are. Fundamentalist Christians in the US, for instance, don't just think of themselves as better Christians, but as the *only* true Christians.

**E.W.** Because they believe that the Bible has an objective interpretation. They are blind to the fact that their interpretation of God is only *one* possible way of understanding Christianity.

**G.L.** And the reason for this lies in the fact that they map strict morality onto their religion. People who apply a Strict Father lens to religion are less aware fact that their faith's scripts can be read in different ways, and the reason for this is really quite straightforward: the strict interpretation says that you have to follow God's word exactly. God is the unquestionable and legitimate moral authority. He came up with certain rules, and we will we get to heaven only if we follow those rules. The *only* way to act morally is to act exactly as God prescribes.

**E.W.** And in order for this equation to work, the rules that tell us specifically how to act have to come directly from God. God's rules can't be up for discussion, just as the strict father's rules are not up for discussion.

**G.L.** Exactly! God's rules can't be subject to different interpretations by believers, just as the strict father's rules are not subject to different interpretations by his children.

Otherwise, how would orderly conduct be maintained? How would we know when behavior is to be punished or rewarded?

**E.W.** God's word simply *must* be objective for the system to function. In a strict family, you follow your father's word and you certainly do *not* entertain your own interpretations of what your father's word might mean. Which makes a purely strict interpretation of religion irreconcilable with the notion that believers are allowed to interpret scripts.

Which implies that if an entire nation were to follow the word of a strict God, then the most "fundamentalist" people would be the good guys, because they stick exactly with what God says.

**G.L.** But if that entire nation were to follow the guidance of a nurturant God, things would look different. In that scenario, those who cared for others, showed them empathy, and nurtured them would be the better Christians.

### 7.6. To Tolerate or Not to Tolerate?
### A question of religious values

**E.W.** And the "better Christians" would also include those who tolerate other religious denominations and orientations.

**G.L.** You bet.

**E.W.** But tolerating other religious groups is commonly seen as a secular and not a religious value.

**G.L.** That's only true if you adapt a strict interpretation of your religion. Because in Strict Father religion, there can only be one legitimate moral authority over mankind, namely your own God. The moment you accept other religions, you are calling into question God's absolute authority and the validity of His rules and commandments. So you need to promote your own religion and defend it against other religions. This is shared by fundamentalist Muslims in the

Middle East, fundamentalist Christians in the US, and ultra-orthodox Jews in Israel.

In the eyes of strict religion, anyone who tolerates other religions is violating a fundamental religious value by questioning God's legitimate authority.

**E.W.** This is an important observation, because nurturant religions often make the mistake of adapting this fundamentalist frame. Many people who share nurturant religious views — many of whom share progressive worldviews — just stand by while their religious beliefs, such as openness towards other religions, are coined and criticized as secular.

**G.L.** But the tolerance of nurturant religion is equally as faithful and God-abiding as the intolerance of strict religion. Tolerating other religions is not a worldly value. It's a religious value.

In progressive religion, tolerating other people and their beliefs is following the word of God. *Not* tolerating others, on the other hand, would be an act against God's will.

**E.W.** So progressive religious groups have not given up on their religion or loosened its moral corset. By being tolerant, they are doing exactly as God expects them to do!

**G.L.** Absolutely. Progressive Christians, for example, are merely trying to live by the standards Jesus set for them — show no violence, offer forgiveness, help the sick and poor, and don't try to dominate others or force your will and beliefs onto them. The idea is that everyone should act by those standards. And if that were fully accomplished, the world would be free of violence, retribution, hate, sickness, poverty, and despair — as well as from domination and intolerance.

**E.W.** But right at this point things get complicated. Let's assume we lived by nurturant religious values. There will always be people that endorse strict religious values. They will not tolerate others, and they will even fight them. I can't help but ask myself: why live by the moral standards that

Jesus taught us if tolerance inescapably leads to social and political domination by those who endorse strict ideals?

**G.L.** Mahatma Gandhi gave an answer to that. "Be the change you want to see in the world."

**E.W.** So now we're back to politics.

**G.L.** We indeed are, and for a simple reason. For Ghandi, progressive religion, and progressive politics are fueled by one and the same moral worldview, namely the Nurturant Parent model.

# Chapter 8

# *Words with No (Single) Meaning*

## *Communication and Contested Concepts*

### 8.1. Two Lands of the Free:
### Why we hear what we think

**E.W.** "In the name of freedom!" is *the* credo of US-American politics. Sometimes, there seems to be quite a bit of friction between ideals and, well, actions. Take, for example, the positions that George W. Bush took during his presidency. He had the US attack Iraq in "Operation Iraqi Freedom." He conducted extensive surveillance on citizens in the name of their liberty. And he rolled back social programs in the name of poor people's liberty to flourish. Under his presidency, some people say, America must have forgotten the meaning of the word "freedom."

**G.L.** Not so. George W. Bush knew *exactly* what the concepts of freedom and liberty meant—to *him*. He attacked Iraq in the name of freedom, and he wholeheartedly believed what he was saying. He spied on people in the name of liberty, and he genuinely believed that it was crucial to take these measures to protect their liberty! He simply held an unapologetically strict, conservative interpretation of freedom and liberty.

It's a big mistake for progressives in the US to think that conservatives are simply misusing words such as "freedom," "liberty," or "fairness" in order to cover up unpleasant or inconvenient truths about their policies. That is naïve and even dangerous. Bush meant exactly what he said when he was pursuing national and international policies "in the name of freedom."

You ask if America has forgotten the meaning of the word "freedom"? No, it hasn't. The problem is a bigger one. America has two entirely different understandings of what "freedom" means—a conservative and a progressive one. And no one talks much about this. So we have to ask ourselves, what does the word "freedom" mean?

**E.W.** Freedom can mean all kinds of things, and even contradictory things. What one person might see as freedom can be viewed and experienced by another as a restriction of freedom.

**G.L.** And they would both be right! Words have no objective meaning. Our conceptual systems lend meaning to words. And these systems can differ based on the experiences we have had, and the worldviews we endorse. We already talked about the fact that people commonly don't realize that the metaphors and frames they use impact their understanding of the world—and words—immensely.

**E.W.** One reason for why we are oblivious to those truths might be the ways in which we construe concepts such as "language," "words," and "communication." Most of us don't realize—and, in fact, never bother to even wonder—how communication really works.

And we use metaphors for communication that make us blind to some very important truths about communication, such as the fact that words can have very different meanings to different people.

**G.L.** I agree. For instance, while not all Americans share the same concept of freedom in their minds, we're inclined to

think they do, and we tend to assume that all people understand words in the same way!

And the reason that we *do* believe that words have
objective meaning has largely to do with our metaphoric
construal of communication. The metaphors we use in our
reasoning about communication make us ignore the fact that
words have no single objective meaning. So, let's ask
ourselves, what is the most common construal of
communication?

## 8.2. *Empty* Words that We Don't *Get*: Metaphors for communication

**E.W.** Easy, one might say. The sender of a message wants to
pass on an idea. So he or she encodes it in terms of a
language system or "code," and passes it on to the receiver.
The receiver then decodes the message — assuming he or she
is fluent in the language being used — and communication is
accomplished.

**G.L.** That's utterly false. It doesn't even come close to
depicting how communication really works! The model
depicts a metaphor that we use to reason about communication, namely the *Communication Is Object Transfer*
metaphor.[43]

**E.W.** This metaphor has an interesting, complex structure.
For one, the act of communicating ideas is understood as
sending *objects* back and forth between interlocutors.

**G.L.** Right, and in order to send *ideas as objects*, we need
containers. Thus, we conceptualize *words as containers* in
which ideas are being transported. We put the ideas into
words, and then we send them off to our addressee.

So there are two mappings inherent to the *Communication
Is Object Transfer* metaphor — *Ideas Are Objects* and *Words Are
Containers*.

---

[43]   Grady 1997, 1998; Reddy 1979; McNeill 1992; Sweetser 1992; Wehling
2010.

**E.W.** Some of the cognitive inferences of these mappings are: in order to send an idea to your interlocutor, you need to find the right container—one that *fits* the idea. You need to find the right words to *transport* your idea. You need to make sure that your interlocutor *receives* the container; that is, you need to make sure he or she can hear or read your words. And so on.

**G.L.** And this metaphor is omnipresent. It shows up in language all the time. We speak of *empty* words, *putting* a lot of meaning *into* our words, and *getting* ideas *across*. We say to people, "You know, you should choose the *content* of your words a bit more carefully," or "I don't get a lot of meaning *out of* what you're saying."

**E.W.** Within this metaphor, the tasks for successful communication are obvious: first, we need to find the right container for our object; that is, the right word for our idea. Then, we need to make sure that the container arrives at its destination; that is, our addressee must be able to see or hear our words. Finally, our addressee has to be able to unpack the container to see what is inside it; that is, he or she must share our language code.

**G.L.** Right. There's an important metaphoric inference to this mapping, and you just named it: we assume that once the words have been *received*, our interlocutor can *unpack* them and will find exactly the meaning that we—the sender—*put into* the package. It is assumed that if we share the same language, the idea I pack up and send to you is the idea you will unpack.

**E.W.** The metaphor construes the meaning of words as independent of their communicative context or the individual's conceptual system. In other words, the metaphor leads us to assume that if we reason about ideas as objects, then they are, well, "objective!"

**G.L.** Yes. Whenever we reason about ideas in this way, we cannot help but infer that they have objective meaning.

Because an object doesn't change its form just because it's being sent somewhere. What I *package up* is what you will *unpack*.

**E.W.** Meaning if I send a box of homemade nougat truffles to my aunt in Germany, she will presumably unpack the exact truffles I packed for her.

**G.L.** And since you send your aunt nougat truffles, she will *not* unpack chocolate-marzipan truffles. She will unwrap the same nougat truffles you packed.

But the idea that communication works like this is complete nonsense! The mere notion that we *transfer* ideas as objects is inapplicable to what we really do as we talk to each other, because the ideas we communicate to others remain in our heads. They don't cease to exist in our reasoning. They're not being taken out of our heads and sent somewhere else.

**E.W.** So, the "problem" with this metaphor, if you will, is that it disregards important facts about the reality of communication. Miscommunication, for instance, is not necessarily caused by choosing the wrong words for our ideas; that is, picking the wrong *containers* for our *objects*. And it's not just caused by our words not successfully being perceived, read, or heard either; that is, it's not that our *containers* didn't make it all the way *across* to our interlocutor. Those things can happen, but they are not the biggest challenge in communication.

**G.L.** The biggest challenge is that words mean different things to different receivers. In reality, words—as containers—*do* carry different contents for different people. The receiver doesn't necessarily *unpack* what the sender *packed*.

**E.W.** When I send nougat truffles to my aunt, she might very well find herself unwrapping chocolate-marzipan truffles.

**G.L.** In fact, chances are she will. The meaning of words is never entirely objective. The words that we receive are being processed through our conceptual systems and the configurations of our brains.

Words do not denote the world as it exists per se. They only denote the way in which we perceive the world based on the biological functioning of our brains.

### 8.3. Embodied Communication: The world in our brains

**E.W.** Now we know how people *think* they communicate but they in fact do not communicate. Let's give our readers a break and tell them how people *do* communicate.

**G.L.** We use our own, individual conceptual systems — our own set of rules for speaking, and our own set of metaphors and frames. And if we happen to speak to someone whose conceptual system largely overlaps with ours, then we can experience shared "reality." The more overlap we have in our rules for speaking, metaphors, and frames, the higher the chances will be that we will understand each other.

**E.W.** You're saying this is about *shared* reality, not *objective* reality?

**G.L.** Humans have no access to realities that lie outside of their perception and are therefore independent of their cognitive processes. We cannot experience realities that objectively exist in the world independent of our human cognitive apparatus. To us, the only reality that exists is the reality that our minds and brains allow us to perceive.

There's a simple reason for that: we have to process the world in order to understand it. Our brains process all incoming information. So the structure of our brains and minds will impact how we *perceive* incoming information.

**E.W.** That's right, our knowledge of the world is always dependent on the workings of our conceptual system.

But hold on, to our readers, this may sound as if we are disputing the existence of a real world and joining the relativist school of thought.

**G.L.** But we aren't, by no means. The world is real, and the ways in which our bodies and conceptual systems process the world are equally real.

It wouldn't cross my mind to contest the notion that the world is real. We all live in this world and interact with it on a daily basis. And our physical, social, and interpersonal experiences in this factually existing world influence our conceptual systems in significant ways. So, cognitive science research is about "embodied realism,"[44] and it belongs neither with strict relativist nor objectivist philosophical schools of thought.

**E.W.** Since people's brains and experiences are similar, we acquire a lot of the same conceptual structures — metaphors, frames, and so on. But we also have experiences that are unique to individuals or groups, for instance those based on the specifics of our bodies,[45] linguistic experiences,[46] and culture.[47]

**G.L.** And such differences in experience lead to differences in the conceptual templates that govern our reasoning.

Some realities are easier to share, because they are based on conceptual structures that all humans acquire. But sometimes it's hard to create shared reality because people don't all share the same experiences in their lives.

But one thing is clear: the world is real, and people understand it through their bodies and brains.

**E.W.** So the theory that words can adequately describe the world as it exists, independent of humans, is a myth.

**G.L.** That theory falls apart the moment you consider embodied metaphoric reasoning. If I say to you, "House prices are on the *rise*," then my words don't actually depict the world as it exists. I employ a metaphor, and this

---

[44]   E.g., Lakoff & Johnson 1999; Johnson & Lakoff 2002.

[45]   E.g., Casasanto & Jasmin 2010; Casasanto 2014.

[46]   E.g., Boroditsky et al. 2003.

[47]   E.g., Meier et al. 2007; Nuñez & Sweetser 2006; Oppenheimer & Trail 2010.

metaphor is the outcome of experiences I have had in this world. In this specific case, it's the experienced correlation of quantity and verticality.

**E.W.** That doesn't explain yet why Americans wouldn't have one shared understanding of common political terms, such as "freedom."

**G.L.** Well, the meaning we attribute to the word "freedom" depends on what frames and metaphors our conceptual system is using. And there is a lot of wiggle room in the way we interpret what "freedom" is, because the concept is essentially contested.

### 8.4. The Never-Ending Semantic Battle: Contested concepts

**E.W.** British social scientist Walter Bryce Gallie first studied Essentially Contested Concepts in 1956.[48] He noticed that abstract ideas such as "democracy" have a core meaning—a semantic skeleton, if you will—but beyond that, they are highly contested. People, Gallie found, interpret these concepts in very different ways.

**G.L.** And over the last decades, cognitive science has looked a bit more into this, and we now have a pretty good idea of how contested concepts work.[49]

Every contested concept has a central meaning, which all people agree upon. This is the uncontested semantic skeleton of the word or idea.

**E.W.** This skeleton dictates a certain structure for the idea, and this central structure remains stable, no matter what conceptual templates an individual brings to the table.

**G.L.** But it's really just a skeletal structure we're talking about, and our individual cognitive apparatuses must complete this structure. The empty semantic slots have to be

---

[48]   Gallie 1956.
[49]   E.g., Schwartz 1992; Lakoff 2006; Lakoff & Wehling 2012.

filled in, and we fill them in based on our beliefs about the world, our values, and our ideals.

Freedom is essentially contested in this way, and people fill in the empty slots in its semantic structure in very different ways. People in America—and elsewhere—have different beliefs, values, and ideals, and therefore their contestation of "freedom" can leave them with entirely different or even contradictory meanings of the word.

**E.W.** But people still concur on the central meaning of the word "freedom."

**G.L.** Yes, at its very inner core, the concept of freedom means the same thing to people. Physical freedom, for instance—the ability to "move freely"—is part of the idea's uncontested core.

**E.W.** In this case, every concept should be essentially contested. Not just "abstract" ideas such as freedom, fairness, or democracy. We always interpret ideas beyond their central meaning based on our knowledge and beliefs.

**G.L.** Well, Gallie's notion of Essentially Contested Concepts only referred to highly abstract ideas, such as the ones we discussed. But the more we study contested concepts, the more evidence there seems to be that ideas are always—in one way or another, and to different degrees—contested.

Let me give you an example. When I first started thinking about Essentially Contested Concepts, I asked myself, "Okay, what about a chair?" I thought about a furniture store in San Francisco that I had been to several times. In that store, there were a bunch of objects that the storeowner called "chairs." Well, not in a hundred years would I have called some of those objects "chairs." If it hadn't been for the context, if they hadn't been offered to me as chairs, they would simply never have been chairs to me. My reality would have remained chairless.

Well, I'm sure that many furniture designers would have recognized these furniture pieces as chairs *right away*.

**E.W.** Because they have different knowledge, beliefs, and values when it comes to chairs, and so they extend the semantic skeleton of the "chair" concept differently.

**G.L.** Or, let's take another example. Until this day, my wife and I disagree over how many rooms there are in our home. There's a space in the house that my wife thinks is a room, and I don't. You get to it through an archway, but there is no door that clearly separates it. I find the case pretty clear that if there's no door, it can't be a room! But my wife thinks that the archway separates the two spaces, leaving us with two rooms, not just one. As you can tell, my wife and I have different contestations of the idea of a "room." In my wife's reality, our home has one more room than I think we have.

**E.W.** Most of the time, though, we don't even notice that we understand concepts differently. We often leave conversations in high spirits thinking that we have gotten our points across successfully, told the other person exactly what we think, and understood what our interlocutor said. While at the same time, we might have completely different understandings of what was said in the conversation! Because we hear only what we *think* was said.

**G.L.** No doubt about it. When we communicate, we each depend on our own minds and brains to extract and construct meaning. And this means we often don't understand exactly "what someone said." We always understand "what we think." We can only understand what our mind *makes* of words by filling in empty semantic slots, evaluating concepts, and interpreting ideas.

**E.W.** Given all these whens and ifs, how can we ever hope to communicate successfully?

**G.L.** We communicate successfully on a regular basis to the extent that concepts have a shared semantic skeleton that our minds can latch onto, and that in fact offers us tangible, "baseline" meaning. Moreover, the more metaphors, frames, and values we share, the more our interpretations along the skeletal structures will look alike and be aligned.

**E.W.** And at this point, successful communication becomes a question of parallelism between interlocutors' metaphors and frames. There are metaphors and frames all people share. Then there are metaphors and frames we share with people from our specific cultures and subcultures. There are metaphors and frames we share with people that speak the same language or dialect that we do. And there are metaphors and frames we share with our close social circles — our intimate friends and family.

The more overlap people have in terms of their life experiences and cultural as well as subcultural exposure, the better fighting chance they have at creating shared meaning. In contrast, if we grow up in different cultures and contexts, then we'll have fewer shared metaphors and frames, and we'll be less likely to interpret concepts in the same way.

**G.L.** Oh yes. Let me tell you a story. One of George W. Bush's staff members, Karen Hughes, was a sort of an unofficial ambassador for the Arab world during his presidency. She would travel to Arab countries to find out what people thought about the US. She gave talks and had conversations with various people. One day, a group of wealthy women in Saudi Arabia invited her to give a talk. When she gave that talk, Hughes said something along the lines of, "My idea of freedom is being able to get into my car and drive to wherever I want. Unfortunately, you don't have this freedom." And the women in the audience were up in arms, "What are you talking about? We can drive anywhere we want, and we even have a driver to take us there. We have more freedom than you do!"

**E.W.** We discussed the fact that people resort to different frames when reasoning about politics based on the world-views they employ. This mechanism is operating when it comes to Essentially Contested Concepts, such as freedom, as well.

**G.L.** That's right. And if you look at the American context, you see that people's different notions of freedom have everything to do with their reasoning in terms of Strict Father and Nurturant Parent morality.

## 8.5. In the Name of Two Freedoms:
### Contested concepts and political communication

**E.W.** Let's discuss the significance of Essentially Contested Concepts for political communication. For one, you can use words like "freedom" without describing what you mean by it exactly—without contextualizing it. You offer your listeners the semantic skeleton of the idea, and let them interpret it in terms of their own values and ideals—with the result that people can project different—and even con-trasting—values onto the idea, believing that theirs are the values that you're advocating.

**G.L.** Exactly. That mechanism is used a lot in politics. It can be quite convenient, especially for short-term effects. When George W. Bush gave his second inauguration speech on January 20, 2005, he used the words "freedom," "free," and "liberty" forty-nine times.[50] About half the time he didn't contextualize them in terms of a conservative worldview. He said things along the lines of, "We need to bring freedom to people around the globe." Conservatives and progressives understood sentences like this one equally as well.

**E.W.** Equally as well, but not in the same way.

**G.L.** Yes. Progressives interpreted his words in terms of a nurturant worldview, and probably said to themselves, "He's right. We need to free people around the globe from despair, intolerance, and violence." Conservatives, however, interpreted the president's words in terms of a strict world-view, thinking, "Right on, Mister President. We must bring people around the globe the freedom to pursue their self-interests in true free market societies."

---

[50]    For a thorough discussion, see Lakoff 2006.

**E.W.** The president was essentially giving two inauguration speeches—one in the minds of progressives, one in the minds of conservatives.

**G.L.** Yes, at least during the first part of his speech. Then he shifted gears and started talking about expanding freedom at home, in the US. From this point on, he talked straight conservative freedom. If you were a progressive at home in front of the TV or radio, you had an interesting experience. From one minute to the next, you no longer knew what the man was talking about. In the second part of the speech, the freedom concept was used in a strictly conservative context, contested in terms of Strict Father values.

What's interesting is that the document George W. Bush was looking at during his speech apparently had markers at exactly those moments where the conservative contestation of freedom was being used. This probably means that whoever wrote the text intended to use the two different meanings of "freedom."

**E.W.** One of the most interesting sentences in George W. Bush's second inauguration speech was, "In America's ideal of freedom, the public interest depends on private character —on integrity, and tolerance toward others, and the rule of conscience in our own lives. Self-government relies, in the end, on the governing of the self."[51]

**G.L.** I agree, that was a remarkable sentence. And as progressives listened to it, they probably asked themselves, "What is that about?"

Well, it was about moral strength and self-discipline. If all US citizens just developed the discipline and strength to look after themselves, the well-being and freedom of all would be maximized.

**E.W.** Another remarkable sentence from that speech was, "By making every citizen an agent of his or her own destiny,

---

[51] "President Sworn-In to Second Term," *The White House*, 1/20/2005: http://www.whitehouse.gov/news/releases/2005/01/20050120-1.html.

we will give our fellow Americans greater freedom from want and fear, and make our society more prosperous and just and equal."[52]

Both statements obviously only make sense within a Strict Father worldview: the only way to free our society from "want and fear" is to incentivize citizens to become completely self-reliant. In order to become sufficiently self-reliant, you need to develop as much self-discipline as you possibly can. To become self-disciplined, you first need to be disciplined by others, through "tough love." Behind this is the idea that governmental intervention, such as social programs and public health care, get in the way of people's freedom.

Society has to remain highly competitive so that everyone can pursue his or her self-interest. Therefore, a well functioning system of social and economic reward and punishment must be in place. Providing people with things they have not earned for themselves creates dependencies, which minimizes their freedom.

**G.L.** And in this worldview, society is better off if people pursue their own interests. It's interesting that George W. Bush used the words "just and equal" in this context. What he means is that society is more "just" if moral strength is rewarded and moral weakness is punished. And society is more "equal" if everyone can compete freely in pursuing their individual well-being—"free" from governmental interventions such as regulations and social welfare.

**E.W.** If you are a progressive, the exact opposite applies. Freeing your fellow citizens from "want and fear" and making our society "more prosperous and just and equal" means to take on responsibility for your fellow Americans by helping to take care of those who need it. For instance, the social welfare system, public health care, good public education are what guarantees equality, prosperity, and freedom from want and fear.

---

[52]   Ibid.

It's remarkable that the US media didn't really discuss the fact that the freedom principles George W. Bush was talking about stood in stark contrast to the progressive notion of freedom that many Americans hold.

**G.L.** Well, some journalists at least talked about the fact that they were quite confused by the speech.

**E.W.** And yet, none of these journalists discussed explicitly the fact that the president used "freedom" to convey conservative societal order.

**G.L.** I don't disagree with you. It's the job of US journalists to recognize what's going on and openly discuss the implications of conflicting interpretations of "American freedom" and the potential fallout for politics and policymaking.

Chapter 9

# *"Once Upon a Time..."*

## The Fairytale of Objective Journalism

### 9.1. Objective Reporting:
### Ideal and reality

**E.W.** Many professional journalists pride themselves in following the rules of objective reporting. But considering what we have discussed thus far, truly "objective" journalism is impossible.

**G.L.** I agree, truly objective communication is impossible on all subject matters and so truly objective journalism is impossible on many social and political issues.

**E.W.** So, in a strict sense, there is no such thing as objective reporting. But there are realities and facts that people perceive in much the same way. For example, people die and you can report on the basic facts of their deaths. Forests burn and you can report on the verifiable facts describing the fires. There are things that people generally agree are objectively "true," independent of their political worldview.

**G.L.** Yes. There are facts that we process largely independent of our moral values, political beliefs, and ideological common sense. These are things that journalists can report on factually, in an "objective" manner, if you will, without an ideological slant. Let's call them the "bare facts."

**E.W.** In the Anglo-Saxon tradition, top-notch journalism requires a clear-cut separation of facts and opinions. Journalists must indicate unmistakably when they're voicing their own opinions or an interpretation of the facts. Moreover, formats that intend to purely inform, such as news reporting, should be free of any evaluation whatsoever.

And technically speaking, journalists *can* provide universally valid, value-free political reporting — if they will just separate the "bare facts" from moral evaluation!

**G.L.** Your equation would only hold true if there were enough value-free words that could be used in political discourse to report on the "bare facts" without inferring a moral interpretation. But the problem is, there is practically no morality-free language in political discourse.

Let's assume an honest, professional US journalist wants to live up to the idea of reporting on a political subject in a strictly factual manner. In all good conscience, he or she follows the rule you just laid out. So far, so good?

Actually, no. He or she will *inevitably* use a word that promotes a conservative or progressive moral interpretation of the issue at hand.

Political reporters in the US and elsewhere are usually unaware that they are using moral language in their reporting. They truly believe that they're being unbiased and impartial.

A while back, I googled the word "tax relief" for a book I was working on. What popped up were about three thousand news reports that used the phrase "tax relief" as if it were a neutral term in the tax debate. That's three thousand articles meant to inform readers of the "objective" facts on the matter of taxation.

**E.W.** While, in actuality, these articles all promoted a conservative moral interpretation of the issue.

**G.L.** Yes. The majority of professional journalists are oblivious to this. They genuinely believe they are reporting in an unbiased manner because they don't understand the mechanisms of political framing.

**E.W.** I think it's time for journalists to realize and take into account in their reporting that the words they are using carry subtle ideological biases. A free, unbiased media needs to be more cognizant of phrases that propagate the ideology of one political camp over the other. Journalists should *report* on the frames that political camps introduce to public discourse.

**G.L.** Ideally, yes. But to do so, they would first have to learn about how relevant framing is, and how it relates to human cognition, democratic discourse, and political action.

### 9.2. The Custodians of Conceptual Freedom: Conscious journalism

**E.W.** Sounds like we're going in circles!

**G.L.** You're right, we are. The political journalists need to catch up with what the science desks are already reporting on.

Moreover, basic cognitive science should be a standard requirement in journalism school. But this is not the case right now. Journalism schools in the US usually don't include cognitive and neuroscience research in their curricula. But it's vital that political journalists understand at least the basics of how political cognition and language work.

**E.W.** In order to be able to account for the ways in which human cognition, including their own reasoning, works.

**G.L.** Yes, they should be able to inform the public on the ways in which language is influencing their political thinking.

**E.W.** So findings on political framing must be taken into account in the work of journalists. Linguistic frames that come along with political programs and platforms must be openly discussed. For instance, journalists should discuss the moral reasoning and worldviews that are transported via certain political phrases, and this should be done in everyday reporting, not just in the occasional opinion pieces.

**G.L.** And to really educate the public on what goes on in politics, journalists should go beyond *calling out* the misleading nature of phrases such as the "War on Terror," which framed a criminal act as an act of warfare.

They should also discuss the worldview that such politically charged terminology fosters in the public mind and the fallout of blindly incorporating this frame in our political reasoning.

After 9/11, for instance, journalists adopted and continued to use the frames employed by the Bush Administration, saying, "Years after the 9/11 attack, the US still finds itself engaged in a War on Terror." Well, they could just as well have reported, "Years after the 9/11 attack, the conservative government still uses the 'War on Terror' *metaphor* to justify its foreign and domestic policies." And then they could have explained the inferences of that metaphor, and how it fits with a strict moral worldview. They could have discussed the hidden realities of the situation, and how use of that metaphor promotes ultraconservative policy as the only policy that's morally right. But in the present context, such reporting would be called "biased."

**E.W.** This type of journalism would be political journalism that has freed itself from the linguistic and conceptual dictates of political parties.

See, journalists are supposed to be the "mirror of society" that ensures self-monitoring of our collective actions and beliefs. And journalists that had some basic knowledge of the workings of the human mind would be better prepared to meet this expectation.

I really think it's high time for journalists in the US and elsewhere to consider neuro- and cognitive science research in their work.

**G.L.** Yes. Some professions take more responsibility than others for keeping public discourse free and transparent. Journalists undoubtedly make part of this group. Journalists have a vital, central job in democracy. They are the keepers of our freedom of information, opinion, and ideas.

**E.W.** And in order to make objectively informed decisions about what we want to support politically, we need to understand the worldviews that underlie the frames being used in daily political debate.

Let me put it this way: we need moral transparency and linguistic plurality in order to secure conceptual plurality.

**G.L.** And it's part of the job of journalists to secure such plurality. It's not an easy job, and I don't envy them for it. But if they want to do it right, they can't simply ignore scientific facts about how language in public debate intersects with cognition and democracy.

**E.W.** Moreover, one of the reasons that metaphors, frames, and Essentially Contested Concepts are so powerful in public discourse is that people remain unaware of the relevance of metaphoric framing in their own cognition and — more specifically — their political decision-making.

**G.L.** Exactly. People don't recognize that the language they're exposed to in the media creates particular realities in their minds. It's astonishing that even the most *basic* findings from fields that study human cognition — such as, neuroscience, cognitive science, and psychology — are not part of our public awareness.

As individuals, we much too readily hand over the power of our own reasoning to politicians, political strategists, and spin doctors who essentially take advantage of our lack of awareness about our own cognition and decision-making.

**E.W.** So securing a more "conscious" journalism is vital for maintaining and fostering truly democratic discourses.

And in order to achieve a more "conscious" journalism, we desperately need to let go of the idea of "objective" journalism, which in fact hinders our journey toward more pluralistic and less biased reporting.

**G.L.** Absolutely. The assumption that "objective" journalism always exists hampers plurality and transparency, especially on social and political issues. We need to let go of that assumption — the sooner the better.

# References

Barsalou, L.W. (2008). Grounded cognition. *Annual Review of Psychology, 59,* 2008, 617–645.

Bergen, B. (2012). *Louder than words: The new science of how the mind makes meaning.* New York: Basic Books.

Boroditsky, L. (2000). Metaphoric structuring: Understanding time through spatial metaphors. *Cognition, 75*(1), 1–28.

Boroditsky, L. (2001). Does language shape thought?: Mandarin and English speakers' conceptions of time. *Cognitive Psychology, 43,* 1–22.

Boroditsky, L., Schmidt, L., & Phillips, W. (2003). Sex, syntax, and semantics. In D. Gentner, & S. Goldin-Meadow (Eds.), *Language in mind: Advances in the study of language and cognition* (pp. 61–79). Cambridge: Cambridge University Press.

Bougher, L.D. (2012). The case for metaphor in political reasoning and cognition. *Political Psychology, 33*(1), 145–163.

Boulenger, V., Hauk, O., & Pulvermüller, F. (2009). Grasping ideas with the motor system: Semantic somatotopy in idiom comprehension. *Cerebral Cortex, 19,* 1905–1914.

Caporale, N., & Dan, Y. (2009). Spike timing-dependent plasticity: A Hebbian learning rule. *Annual Review of Neuroscience, 31,* 25–46.

Casasanto, D., & Jasmin, K. (2010). Good and bad in the hands of politicians: Spontaneous gestures during positive and negative speech. *PLoS ONE, 5*(7), e11805.

Casasanto, D. (2014). Bodily relativity. In L. Shapiro (Ed.), *Routledge handbook of embodied cognition* (pp. 108–117). New York: Routledge.

Charteris-Black, J. (2005). *Politicians and rhetoric: The persuasive power of metaphor.* Basingstoke: Palgrave Macmillan.

Cienki, A. (2005). The metaphorical use of family terms versus other nouns in political discourse. *Information Design Journal and Document Design, 13*(1), 27–39.

Citron, F., & Goldberg, A. (2014). Metaphorical sentences are more emotionally engaging than their literal counterparts. *Journal of Cognitive Neuroscience, 26*(11), 2585–2595.

Croft, W., & Cruse, D.A. (2004). *Cognitive linguistics.* Cambridge: Cambridge University Press.

Desai, R., Binder, J., Contant, L., & Seidenberg, M. (2010). Activation of sensory-motor areas in sentence comprehension. *Cerebral Cortex, 20*(2), 468–478.

Desai, R., Binder, J., Conant, L., Mano, Q., & Seidenberg, M. (2011). The neural career of sensory-motor metaphors. *Journal of Cognitive Neuroscience, 23*, 2376–2386.

Ekman, P. & Friesen, W.V. (1969). The repertoire of nonverbal behavior: Categories, origins, usage, and coding. *Semiotica, 1*(1), 49–98.

Ekman, P. (1985). *Telling lies.* New York: Berkeley Books.

Feinberg, M., & Wehling, E. (2016) A moral house divided: How idealized family models impact political cognition. *Submitted.*

Fillmore, C. (1976). Frame semantics and the nature of language. In R. Stevan, H. Harnad, D. Steklis, & J. Lancaster (Eds.), *Origins and evolution of language and speech*, Vol. 280 (pp. 20–32). New York: Annals of the NY Academy of Sciences.

Fillmore, C. (1985). Frames and the semantics of understanding. *Quaderni di Semantica, 6*, 222–254.

Foroni, F., & Semin, G.R. (2013). Comprehension of action negation involves inhibitory simulation. *Frontiers in Human Neuroscience, 7*, 209.

Gallese, V., Fadiga, L., Fogassi, L., & Rizzolatti, G. (1996). Action recognition in the premotor cortex. *Brain, 119*(2), 593–609.

Gallese, V. (1999). The 'shared manifold' hypothesis: From mirror neurons to empathy. *Journal of Consciousness Studies, 8*(5–7), 33–50.

Gallese, V., & Lakoff, G. (2005). The brain's concepts: The role of the sensory-motor system in conceptual knowledge. *Cognitive Neuropsychology, 22*(3), 455–479.

Gallie, W. (1956). Essentially contested concepts. *Proceedings of the Aristotelian Society, 56*, 167–198.

Gamez-Djokic, V., Narayanan, S., Wehling, E., Sheng, T., Bergen, B., Davis, J., & Aziz-Zadeh, L. (2015). Morally queasy: Metaphors implying moral disgust activate specific subregions of the insula and basal ganglia. *Submitted.*

Gibbs, R.W. (1996). Why many concepts are metaphorical. *Cognition, 61*, 309–319.

Gibbs, R.W. (2006). *Embodiment and cognitive science.* Cambridge: Cambridge University Press.

Goffman, E. (1974). *Frame analysis: An easy on the organization of experience.* Cambridge, MA: Harvard University Press.

Grady, J. (1997). *Foundations of meaning: Primary metaphors and primary scenes.* Doctoral Thesis, University of California, Berkeley.

Grady, J. (1998). The conduit metaphor revisited: A reassessment of metaphors for communication. In J.-P. Koenig (Ed.), *Discourse and cognition: Bridging the gap* (pp. 205–218). Stanford, CA: CSLI Publications.

Hebb, D.O. (1949). *The organization of behavior.* New York: Wiley.

Higgins, E.T. (1996). Knowledge activation: Accessibility, applicability, and salience. In E.T. Higgins, & A.W. Kruglanski (Eds.), *Social psychology: Handbook of basic principles* (pp. 133–168). New York: Guilford.

Johnson, M. (1987). *The body in the mind: The bodily basis of meaning, imagination and reason.* Chicago: University of Chicago Press.

Johnson, C. (1997). Metaphor vs. conflation in the acquisition of polysemy: The case of see. In M.K. Hiraga, C. Sinha, & S. Wilcox (Eds.), *Cultural, typological and psychological perspectives in cognitive linguistics* (pp. 155–169). Amsterdam: John Benjamins.

Johnson, M. & Lakoff, G. (2002). Why cognitive linguistics requires embodied realism. *Cognitive Linguistics, 13*(3), 245–263.

Kahneman, D., & Tversky, A. (1984). Choices, values, and frames. *American Psychologist, 39*(4), 1984, 341–350.

Kaup, B., Lüdtke, J., & Zwaan, R.A. (2006). Processing negated sentences with contradictory predicates: Is a door open that is mentally closed? *Journal of Pragmatics, 38*, 1033–1050.

Kaup, B., Yaxley, R.H., Madden, C.J., Zwaan, R.A., & Lüdtke, J. (2007). Experiential simulations of negated text information. *Quarterly Journal of Experimental Psychology, 60*, 976–990.

Lacey, S., Stilla, R., & Sathian, K. (2012). Metaphorically feeling: Comprehending textural metaphors activates somatosensory cortex. *Brain and Language, 120*(3), 416–421.

Lakoff, G. (1987a). Cognitive models and prototype theory. In U. Neisser (Ed.), *Concepts and conceptual development: Ecological and intellectual factors in categorization* (pp. 63–100). New York: Cambridge University Press.

Lakoff, G. (1987b). *Women, fire and dangerous things: What categories tell us about the nature of thought*. Chicago: University of Chicago Press.

Lakoff, G., & Johnson, M. (1980). *Metaphors we live by*. Chicago: University of Chicago Press.

Lakoff, G. (1996). *Moral politics: How conservatives and liberals think*. Chicago: University of Chicago Press.

Lakoff, G., & Johnson, M. (1999). *Philosophy in the flesh: The embodied mind and its challenge to Western thought*. New York: Basic Books.

Lakoff, G. (2003, 3/18) Metaphor and War, Again. *AlterNet*. Retrieved from: http://www.alternet.org/story/15414/

Lakoff, G. (2004). *Don't think of an elephant!: Know your values and frame the debate*. White River Junction: Chelsea Green.

Lakoff, G. (2006). *Whose freedom?: The battle over America's most important idea*. New York: Farrar, Straus and Giroux.

Lakoff, G., & Wehling, E. (2012). *The little blue book: The essential guide to thinking and talking Democratic*. New York: Simon and Schuster.

Landau, M.J., Sullivan, D., & Greenberg, J. (2009). Evidence that self-relevant motives and metaphoric framing interact to influence political and social attitudes. *Psychological Science, 20*(11), 1421–1427.

Matlock, T. (2004). Fictive motion as cognitive simulation. *Memory and Cognition, 32*(8), 1389–1400.

McNeill, D. (1992). *Hand and mind: What gestures reveal about thought*. Chicago: University of Chicago Press.

Meier, B., Hauser, D., Robinson, M., Friesen, C., & Schjeldahl, K. (2007). What's up with God?: Vertical space as a representation of the divine. *Journal of Personality and Social Psychology, 93*(5), 699–710.

Miller, D. (1999). The norm of self-interest. *American Psychologist, 54*, 1053–1060.

Minsky, M. (1974). A framework for representing knowledge. Memorandum, 306, AI Laboratory, Massachusetts Institute of Technology.

Moeller, S., Robinson, M., & Zabelina, D. (2008). Personality dominance and preferential use of the vertical dimension of space: Evidence from spatial attention paradigms. *Psychological Science, 19*, 355–361.

Musolff, A. (2004). *Metaphor and political discourse: Analogical reasoning in debates about Europe.* Basingstoke: Palgrave Macmillan.

Musolff, A. (2006). Metaphor scenarios in public discourse. *Metaphor and Symbol, 21*(1), 23–38.

Niedenthal, P.M., Barsalou, L.W., Winkielman, P., Krauth-Gruber, S., & Ric, F. (2005). Embodiment in attitudes, social perception, and emotion. *Personality and Social Psychology Review, 9*(3), 184–211.

Nuñez, R., & Sweetser, E. (2006). With the future behind them: Convergent evidence from Aymara language and gesture in the crosslinguistic comparison of spatial construals of time. *Cognitive Science, 30*, 401–450.

Oppenheimer, D., & Trail, T. (2010). Why leaning to the left makes you lean to the left: Effect of spatial orientation on political attitudes. *Social Cognition, 28*(5), 651–661.

Pulvermüller, F. (2001). Brain reflections of words and their meaning. *Trends in Cognitive Sciences, 5*(12), 517–524.

Pulvermüller, F. (2002). *The neuroscience of language.* Cambridge: Cambridge University Press.

Ratner, R.K., & Miller, D.T. (2001). The norm of self-interest and its effects on social action. *Journal of Personality and Psychology Research, 81*(1), 5–16.

Reddy, M. (1979). The conduit metaphor. In A. Ortony (Ed.), *Metaphor and thought* (pp. 284–324). Cambridge: Cambridge University Press.

Rizzolatti, G., Fadiga, L., Gallese, V., & Fogassi, L. (1996). Research report premotor cortex and the recognition of motor actions. *Cognitive Brain Research, 3*(2), 131–141.

Rizzolatti, G., Fogassi, L., & Gallese, V. (2000). Cortical mechanisms subserving object grasping and action recognition: A new view on the cortical motor functions. In M. Gazzaniga (Ed.), *The cognitive neurosciences,* Second Edition (pp. 539–552). Cambridge, MA: MIT Press.

Rizzolatti, G., Fadiga, L., Fogassi, L., & Gallese, V. (2001). From mirror neurons to imitation: Facts and speculations. In W. Prinz, & A. Meltzoff (Eds.), *The imitative mind: Development, evolution and brain bases* (pp. 143–162). Cambridge: Cambridge University Press.

Rock, A. (2005). *The mind at night: The new science of how and why we dream.* New York: Basic Books.

Schlesinger, M., & Lau, R.R. (2000). The meaning and measure of policy metaphors. *American Political Science Review, 94*(3), 611–626.

Schubert, T. (2005). Your highness: Vertical positions as perceptual symbols of power. *Journal of Personality and Social Psychology, 89,* 1–21.

Schwartz, A. (1992). *Contested concepts in cognitive social science.* Honors Thesis, University of California, Berkeley.

Sears, D., & Funk, C. (1991). The role of self-interest in social and political attitudes. In M. Zanna (Ed.), *Advances in experimental social psychology, 2* (pp. 2–94). New York: Academic Press.

Shatz, C.J. (1992). The developing brain. *Scientific American, 267*(3), 60–67.

Shingles, R.D. (1989). Class, status, and support for government aid to disadvantaged groups. *Journal of Politics, 51,* 933–962.

Stanfield, R.A., & Zwaan, R.A. (2001). The effect of implied orientation derived from verbal context on picture recognition. *Psychological Science, 121,* 153–156.

Stec, K., & Sweetser, E. (2013). Borobudur and Chartres: Religious spaces as performative real-space blends. In R. Caballero, & J.E. Díaz Vera (Eds.), *Sensuous cognition: Explorations into human sentience: Imagination, (e)motion and perception* (pp. 265–292). De Gruyter Mouton. 10.1515/9783110300772.

Sweetser, E. (1992). English metaphors for language: Motivations, conventions, and creativity. *Poetics Today, 13*(4): Aspects of Metaphor and Comprehension, 705–724.

Tettamanti, M., Buccino, G., Saccuman, M.C., Gallese, V., Danna, M., Scifo, P., Fazio, F., Rizzolatti, G., Cappa, S.F., & Perani, D. (2005). Listening to action-related sentences activates fronto-parietal motor circuits. *Journal of Cognitive Neuroscience, 17*(2), 273–281.

Tettamanti, M., Manenti, R., Della Rosa, P.A., Falini, A., Perani, D., Cappa, S.F., & Moro, A. (2008). Negation in the brain: Modulating action representations. *Neuroimage, 43*(2), 358–367.

Thibodeau, P., & Boroditsky, L. (2011). Metaphors we think with: The role of metaphor in reasoning. *PLoS ONE, 6*(2), e16782.

Tomasino, B., Weiss, P.H., & Fink, G.R. (2010). To move or not to move: Imperatives modulate action-related verb processing in the motor system. *Neuroscience, 169,* 246–258.

Wehling, E. (2010). Argument is gesture war: Function, form and prosody of discourse structuring gestures in political argument.

*Proceedings of the 35th Annual Meeting of the Berkeley Linguistics Society* (pp. 54–65). Berkeley, CA: Berkeley Linguistics Society.

Wehling, E. (2013). *A nation under joint custody: How conflicting family models divide US-politics.* Doctoral Thesis, University of California at Berkeley.

Wehling, E., Feinberg, M., Chung, J.M., Saslow, L., Malvaer, I., & Lakoff, G. (2015). The Moral Politics Scale: The values behind conservatism, liberalism, and the middle. *Unpublished manuscript.*

Yaxley, R.H., & Zwaan, R.A. (2007). Simulating visibility during language comprehension. *Cognition, 105*(1), 229–236.

Zhong, C.-B., & Liljenquist, K. (2006). Washing away your sins: Threatened morality and physical cleansing. *Science, 313*, 1451–1452.

Zwaan, R.A., Stanfield, R.A., & Yaxley, R.H. (2002). Language comprehenders mentally represent the shape of objects. *Psychological Science, 13*, 168–171.

Zwaan, R.A., & Pecher, D. (2012). Revisiting mental simulation in language comprehension: Six replication attempts. *PLOS One, 7*(12), e51382.

CPSIA information can be obtained
at www.ICGtesting.com
Printed in the USA
LVOW13s1738080617

537419LV00011B/288/P